HARVARD–YENCHING INSTITUTE STUDIES XXV

Kakhun, Sŏk, 13th cent., comp.

LIVES OF EMINENT

KOREAN MONKS

The *Haedong Kosŭng Chŏn*

TRANSLATED WITH AN INTRODUCTION BY

Peter H. Lee

HARVARD UNIVERSITY PRESS

Cambridge, Massachusetts

1969

© Copyright 1969 by the Harvard-Yenching Institute
Distributed in Great Britain by Oxford University Press, London
Library of Congress Catalog Card Number 69–18037
SBN 674–53662–2
Printed in the United States of America

for C. Y. L. and C. S. L.

Foreword

This volume, the twenty-fifth of the Harvard-Yenching Institute Studies, is financed from the residue of the funds granted during World War II by the Rockefeller Foundation for the publication of Chinese and Japanese dictionaries. This series is distinct from the Harvard-Yenching Institute Monograph Series and consists primarily of bibliographical studies, grammars, reference works, translations, and other study and research aids.

Preface

The text I have used in translating *Lives of Eminent Korean Monks* is that in the *Taishō Tripiṭaka*, not because it is a basic text, for it is marred by wrong punctuation and by textual errors, but because it is readily available in major libraries. The earliest available edition in block prints is said to have existed until the outbreak of the Korean War (some say even the blocks themselves existed in Suwŏn, at the Yongju monastery, before 1950); it is now lost. In view of the absence of such an authentic text, I have collated all the versions available to me: among them the manuscript copy of the late Asami Rintarō and the texts in the *Pulgyo, Dainihon bukkyō zensho*, and *Chosŏn pulgyo t'ongsa*. Such collating, together with necessary emendations for puzzling passages, is indicated in footnotes. Ideally, however, a correct text, with all errors eliminated but with collation and emendations, should accompany the translation; but owing to technical difficulties such a text must await another occasion.

This study was completed under a grant from the American Philosophical Society and the University of Hawaii Research Council, and I am grateful to both institutions for their assistance. I am also indebted to Professors Fang Chao-ying, Richard B. Mather, Joseph Needham, and Johannes Rahder for answering my queries; and to Professors Chow Tse-tsung, Masatoshi Naga-tomi, Richard H. Robinson, Edward W. Wagner, and Arthur F. Wright for reading the translation and offering constructive criticism. To Professor Leon Hurvitz go my deep thanks for going over with me the moot points in the texts. However, I alone am responsible for any errors which may remain.

The substance of the Introduction was first presented as a paper before the eighteenth annual meeting of the Association for Asian Studies on April 5, 1966.

Honolulu, Hawaii   Peter H. Lee
September 1968

Contents

Abbreviations

A Asami Rintarō's manuscript copy in Berkeley, Calif.

AM *Asia Major*.

BD Herbert A. Giles. *A Chinese Biographical Dictionary* (Shanghai, 1898).

BEFEO *Bulletin de l' Ecole Française d' Extrême-Orient*.

BHSD Franklin Edgerton. *Buddhist Hybrid Sanskrit Grammar and Dictionary* (New Haven, 1953).

BKD Ono Gemmyō, ed. *Bussho kaisetsu daijiten* (12 vols.; Tokyo, 1933–1936).

CG *Chōsen gakuhō*.

CH *Chindan hakpo*.

Chavannes (1) *Mémoires composé à l'epoque de la grande dynastie T'ang sur les religieux éminents qui allèrent chercher la loi dans les pays d'occident* (Paris, 1894).

Chavannes (2) "Voyages de Song Yun dans l'Udyāna et le Gandhāra (518–522 p.C.)," *BEFEO*, 3 (1903), 379–429.

Chavannes (3) "Les pays d'Occident d'après le *Wei Lio*," *TP*, 6 (1905), 519–571.

Chavannes (4) "Les pays d'Occident d'après le *Heou Han chou*," *TP*, 8 (1907), 149–234.

Chavannes (5) "Seng Houei," *TP*, 10 (1909), 199–212.

CJS *Chōsen jisatsu shiryō* 朝鮮寺利史料 (2 vols.; Keijō, 1911).

CKK Chōsen kosho kankōkai 朝鮮古書刊行會 edition.

CKS *Chōsen kinseki sōran* 朝鮮金石總覽 (2 vols.; Keijō, 1919).

CMP Pak Yong-dae 朴容大 et al. *Chŭngbo munhŏn pigo* 增補文獻備考 (*KKH*; Seoul, 1957).

CPT Yi Nŭng-hwa. *Chosŏn pulgyo t'ongsa* (2 vols.; Seoul, 1918).

CSTCC *Ch'u san-ts'ang chi-chi* (*T.* 55, no. 2145).

HBGR *Hōbōgirin: Dictionnaire Encyclopédique du Bouddhisme d'après les sources chinoises et japonaises* (Tokyo, 1929–1931).

HJAS *Harvard Journal of Asiatic Studies*.

HKC *Haedong kosŭng chŏn* (*T.* 50, no. 2065).

HKSC Tao-hsüan. *Hsü kao-seng chuan* (*T.* 50, no. 2060).

HTS *Hsin T'ang shu* (*Erh-shih-wu shih* edition).

Hurvitz Léon Hurvitz, tr. Wei Shou, *Treatise on Buddhism and Taoism* (ed., Tsukamoto Zenryū), in *Yün-Kang*, XVI, supplement (Kyoto, 1956).

JA *Journal Asiatique*.

JAOS *Journal of the American Oriental Society*.

JAS *Journal of Asian Studies*.

KHMC *Kuang hung-ming chi* (*T.* 52, no. 2103).

Kim Tong-hwa (1) "Koguryŏ sidae ŭi pulgyo sasang," *Asea yŏn'gu*, 2 (1959), 1–44.

Kim Tong-hwa (2) "Silla sidae ŭi pulgyo sasang," *Asea yŏn'gu*, 5 (1962), 1–57.

KKH Kojŏn kanhaeng hoe 古典刊行會 edition (Seoul).

KRS   Chǒng In-ji et al. *Koryǒ sa* 高麗史 (Tongbanghak yǒn'guso 東方學硏究所 edition; Seoul, 1955–1961).

KRSCY   *Koryǒsa chǒryo* 高麗史節要 (*KKH;* Seoul, 1960).

KS   Maema Kyōsaku. *Kosen sappu* (3 vols.; Tokyo, 1944–1957).

KSC   Hui-chiao. *Liang kao-seng chuan* (*T.* 50, no. 2059).

KT   *Korean Tripiṭaka* (Seoul, 1957–).

Lamotte   Étienne Lamotte. *Le Traité de la Grande Vertu de Sagesse de Nāgārjuna* (2 vols.; Louvain, 1944–1949).

Legge   James Legge. *The Chinese Classics* (5 vols.; reprinted, Hong Kong, 1960).

LTSPC   *Li-tai san-pao chi* (*T.* 49, no. 2034).

Maspero (1)   "Le songe et l'ambassade de l'empereur Ming: Étude critique des Sources," *BEFEO*, 10 (1910), 95–130.

Maspero (2)   "Communautés et moines bouddhistes chinois aux 2e et 3e siècles," *BEFEO*, 10 (1910), 222–232.

Maspero (3)   "Les origines de la communauté bouddhiste de Lo-yang," *JA*, 225 (1934), 87–107.

Maspero (4)   *Mélanges posthumes sur les religions et l'histoire de la Chine* (3 vols.; Paris, 1960).

MBD   Mochizuki Shinkō. *Bukkyō daijiten* (10 vols.; Tokyo, 1960–1963).

MCB   *Mélange Chinois et Bouddhiques.*

MH   Édouard Chavannes. *Les mémoires historiques de Se-ma Ts'ien* (5 vols.; Paris, 1895–1905).

MT   Morohashi Tetsuji, ed. *Dai kanwa jiten* (13 vols.; Tokyo, 1955–1960).

MTB   *Memoirs of the Research Department of the Toyo Bunko.*

Pelliot (1)   "Deux itinéraires de Chine en Inde à la fin du VIIIe siècle," *BEFEO*, 4 (1904), 131–413.

Pelliot (2)   "Les *kouo-che* ou maîtres du royaume dans le bouddhisme chinois," *TP*, 12 (1911), 671–676.

Pelliot (3)   "L'origine du nom de 'Chine'," *TP*, 13 (1912), 727–742.

Pelliot (4)   "Encore à propos du nom de 'Chine'," *TP*, 14 (1913), 427–428.

Pelliot (5)   "Les noms propres dans les traductions chinoises du Milindapañha," *JA*, 11 series, 4 (1914), 379–419.

Pelliot (6)   "Meou-tseu ou les doutes levés," *TP*, 19 (1918–1919), 255–433.

Pelliot (7)   "Encore un mot à propos du Sūtra des Causes et des Effets et de l'expression siang-kiao," *TP*, 25 (1927–1928), 92–94; and "Le terme de siang-kiao comme désignation du bouddhisme," *TP*, 26 (1929), 51–52.

Pelliot (8)   *Notes on Marco Polo* (Paris, 1959).

SG   *Seikyū gakusō.*

SGSG   Kim Pu-sik 金富軾. *Samguk sagi* 三國史記 (Chōsen shigakkai edition; Keijō, 1928).

SGYS   Iryǒn 一然. *Samguk yusa* 三國遺事 (Ch'oe Nam-sǒn edition; Seoul, 1954).

SH   Soothill and Hodous, *A Dictionary of Chinese Buddhist Terms* (London, 1937).

SKSC   Tsan-ning. *Sung kao-seng chuan* (*T.* 50, no. 2061).

SPPY   *Ssu-pu pei-yao.*

SPTK   *Ssu-pu tsʻung-kʻan.*

SR   *Shirin.*

SZ   *Shigaku zasshi.*

T   *Taishō shinshū daizōkyō* (100 vols.; Tokyo 1924–1934).

TG   *Tōyō gakuhō.*

TP   *Tʻoung Pao.*

TSCC   *Tʻu-shu chi-chʻeng.*

Tsukamoto   *Gisho Shakurōshi no kenkyū* (Kyoto, 1961).

TYS   No Sa-sin et al. *Sinjŭng Tongguk yŏji sŭngnam* 新增東國輿地勝覽 (*KKH;* Seoul, 1958).

WYWK   *Wan-yu wen-kʻu.*

Yang   Yang Chu-dong. *Kukhak yŏnʻgu nonʻgo* 國學硏究論攷 (Seoul, 1962).

YSGYS   Yi Pyŏng-do. *Wŏnmun pyŏng yŏkchu Samguk yusa* 原文幷譯註三國遺事 (Seoul, 1956).

Zürcher   Erik Zürcher. *The Buddhist Conquest of China: The Spread and Adaptation of Buddhism in Early Medieval China* (2 vols.; Leiden, 1959).

LIVES OF EMINENT

KOREAN MONKS

The *Haedong Kosŭng Chŏn*

INTRODUCTION

The *Haedong kosŭng chŏn*[1] 海東高僧傳 or *Lives of Eminent Korean Monks* is the only extant book of its kind in Korea. The book was compiled by royal command in 1215 by Kakhun[2] 覺訓, abbot of the Yŏngt'ong monastery[3] 靈通寺 in the capital of Koryŏ 高麗, and it was used by Iryŏn[4] 一然 as one

---

1 In using the term *kosŭng* ("eminent monks"), Kakhun is following the example of Hui-chiao, who distinguished "eminent" from "famous": "If men of real achievement conceal their brilliance, then they are eminent but not famous. . . . " See *KSC*, 14, 419a 22–26, and Arthur F. Wright, "Hui-chiao's *Lives of Eminent Monks*," in *Silver Jubilee Volume of the Zinbun Kagaku Kenkyūjo* of Kyoto University (Kyoto, 1954), pp. 407–408.

2 Little is known of this scholar monk, except that he was a friend of such famous writers of Koryŏ as Yi Il-lo 李仁老 (1150–1220; *KRS*, 102, 10a–b), Yi Kyu-bo 李奎報 (1168–1241; *KRS*, 23, 35b, and 102, 3a–5b), and Ch'oe Cha 崔滋 (1188–1260; *KRS*, 25, 17b–18a, and 102, 14b–16a). Yi Il-lo reports, in the *P'ahan chip* 破閑集 (1964 ed.), 2, 39, that Kakhun often likened himself to Li I-chi 酈食其, styling himself "a bald drunkard of Kao-yang" 高陽醉髡; Yi also comments that Kakhun's poetry resembled that of Chia Tao 賈島 (779–843), a T'ang monk who returned to laity and was the author of a collection of verse, *Ch'ang-chiang chi* 長江集 (*Ssu-k'u ch'uan-shu ts'ung-mu*, 150, 8a–b). In fine, Kakhun was a literary monk, immensely popular among contemporary men of letters, especially among seven writers known as the "Seven Sages of the Kangjwa" 江左七賢 who compared themselves to the "Seven Sages of the Bamboo Grove" and indulged in elegant pleasure (for more on these poets see n. 150 to the translation). For more on Kakhun see *P'ahan chip*, 2, 39–40; *Tongguk Yisangguk chip* 東國李相國集 (1958 ed.), 16, 5a; *Pohan chip* 補閑集 (*CKK*), 3, 154–156; *CPT*, I, 5–7; *Tongguk sŭngni rok* 東國僧尼錄, in *Zokuzōkyō*, IIB, 23/3, 347c–d; *SGYS*, Introduction, pp. 29–31. For Chia Tao's verse see Ogawa Tamaki 小川環樹, *Tōshi gaisetsu* (Tokyo, 1958), pp. 68–70; for a brief biographical notice see A. R. Davis, ed., *The Penguin Book of Chinese Verse* (Harmondsworth, 1965), p. 23, and *HTS*, 176, 4052b; for translation of his poem see Robert Payne, ed., *The White Pony* (London, 1949), p. 242, and Witter Bynner, *The Jade Mountain* (New York, 1929), p. 12. For Li I-chi see *Shih chi*, 97, 0228b ff.; *Ch'ien Han shu*, 43, 0464d–0465b; Burton Watson, *Records of the Grand Historian of China* (New York, 1961), I, 283, n. 6. For the expression "kangjwa" (chiang-tso in Chinese) see *JAOS*, 82 (1962), 383.

3 On Mount Ogwan 五冠山, thirty *ri* west of Changdan 長湍. Once the most famous monastery in the Koryŏ capital, it is no longer extant. See *TYS*, 12, 9b–10b. According to the *Chunggyŏng chi* 中京誌 (*CKK*, 1911), 6, 269, it was on Mount Puso 扶蘇山.

4 See *SGYS*, Introduction by Ch'oe Nam-sŏn, and the somewhat antiquated essay by Imanishi Ryū in *Geimon*, 9 (1918), 601–616.

of his primary sources for the compilation of the *Samguk yusa*[5] 三國遺事 in or about 1285. The *Lives*, lost for almost seven centuries, was known only by title and by a few quotations. The book became known to the academic world with the discovery in the early part of this century[6] of a manuscript which contains only the first two chapters, on propagators of the faith.[7] It is not known by what happy chance the book came to be preserved, but we have at least the discoverer's name. He was Yi Hoe-gwang[8] 李晦光 (1840–1911), abbot of the famous Haein monastery[9] 海印寺, the repository of the wood

---

5   See *Geimon*, 9 (1918), 749–761. *SGYS* quotes or comments on a biography of eminent monks as simply *Sŭngjŏn* 僧傳 (3, 121, 127, 128; 5, 215, 231), as *Kosŭng chŏn* (3, 122; 5, 233), or *Haedong sŭngjŏn* 海東僧傳 (4, 184 and 187). Unless Iryŏn is referring to the biography of monks compiled by Kim Tae-mun 金大問 (*SGSG*, 46, 6), which existed at the time of the compilation of *SGSG*, he must be referring to *KSC*. See *SGYS*, Introduction, pp. 29–30. The *Taegak kuksa munjip* 大覺國師 文集 (1931), 16, 4b8, mentions *Haedong sŭngjŏn*, possibly that by Kim but definitely not the compilation of Kakhun.

6   This must have been in or about 1914. The manuscript copy once owned by Asami Rintarō 淺見倫太郎, now in the Asami Collection in Berkeley, Calif., has the following colophon: "Paek Tu-yong 白斗鏞 obtained it at the Hallam sŏrim 翰南書林 on April 25, 1914. On February 15, 1917, I compared and collated my copy with that of Watanabe Akira 渡邊彰." The Asami copy consists of 29 sheets, 10 lines to a page, 19–20 letters to a line.

7   The number of chapters in *HKC* is a matter for conjecture, but internal evidence makes it certain that there were more than two. For instance, Kakhun promises us a biography of Anham (1019c29), and it is in fact in chap. 2, but in 1019c7 he refers us to a biography of Chajang which cannot be found in the extant two chapters. The *Pulgyo*, 46–47 (April-May 1928), 57b, suggests, without documentation, that there were ten chapters.

8   This information is in the Introduction to *HKC* by Ch'oe Nam-sŏn, in the *Changwoe chamnok* 藏外雜錄, I (Seoul, 1956), p. 66. Yi Hoe-gwang was active, from about 1908, in the reform movement of the Korean Buddhist Church. In March 1908, fifty-two Buddhist representatives met and established the Wŏnjong chongmuwŏn 圓宗宗務院 in the Wŏnhŭng monastery, outside the East Gate in Seoul, in the hope of uniting and reforming the Korean church. At the meeting Yi was elected as the Taejongjŏng 大宗正. In September 1910 he went to Japan with credentials signed by seventy-two monasteries, and on October 6 signed a document pledging the merging of the Korean church with that of the Sōtō sect of Japan. But soon opposition arose, especially from the monks in Chŏlla and Kyŏngsang provinces, headed by Pak Han-yŏng 朴漢永 (1870–1948) of the Paegyang monastery 白羊寺 in South Chŏlla, Han Yong-un 韓龍雲 (1879–1944) of the Pŏmŏ monastery 梵魚寺, and Chin Chin-ŭng 陳震應 (1873–1941) of the Hwaŏm monastery 華嚴寺. They in turn organized the opposing Imje (Lin-ch'i) sect. With the promulgation of the ordinance on the Korean Buddhist Church by the Governor-General in June 1911, however, this struggle was brought to a lull. See Yoshikawa Buntarō 吉川文太郎, *Chōsen no shūkyō* (Keijō, 1921), pp. 67–69, a short notice of Yi with his portrait; Takahashi Tōru 高橋亨, *Richō bukkyō* 李朝佛教 (Tokyo, 1929), pp. 920–941; and *CPT*, II, 620–626.

9   Built in 802 on Mount Kaya 伽倻山, near Hapch'ŏn kun 陝川郡, North Kyŏngsang Province. It was one of the three major monasteries in Korea. *TYS*, 30 ,31a-22a; *CJS*, I, 493–500; *Kuksa taesajŏn*, II, 1700a–b.

blocks for the *Korean Tripiṭaka*, and it is said that he found the manuscript at a certain monastery in Sŏngju[10] 星州 in the southwest of North Kyŏngsang Province. The manuscript was immediately reproduced by the Kwangmun hoe[11] 光文會 and circulated among specialists. In 1917 it was published in the *Dainihon bukkyō zensho*, Yūhōden series 2. A year later, in his *History of Korean Buddhism* 朝鮮佛教通史, Yi Nǔng-hwa 李能和 (1868–1945) offered a number of corrections. The late Ch'oe Nam-sŏn 崔南善 (1890–1957) published his critical edition in the magazine *Pulgyo* 佛敎, no. 37 (July 1927).[12] It was also included in the *Taishō Tripiṭaka* (L, no. 2065). Unfortunately, however, no studies have been made,[13] in Korean or any other language, of this invaluable document.

The two extant chapters of the *Lives* contain eighteen major and seven minor biographies of eminent monks and cover a span of five hundred years. The first chapter, which deals with three Koguryŏ monks, two Silla monks, and three monks of foreign origin, is the more important of the two. It throws new and often brilliant light on the development of Korean Buddhism from the time of its introduction to the seventh century. The second chapter, dealing with Silla monks who went to China or India, consists chiefly of excerpts from the *Hsü kao-seng chuan* and from the *Ta-T'ang hsi-yü ch'iu-fa kao-seng chuan* 大唐西域求法高僧傳 (ca. 705) of I-ching[14] 義淨 (635–713), except for the life of the monk Anham 安含, an account found nowhere else.

---

10 Southwest of North Kyŏngsang. Originally Sŏngsan kaya 星山伽倻, one of the six members of the Kaya confederation. Silla conquered Kaya and established Ponp'i hyŏn 本彼縣. Its name was changed by King Kyŏngdŏk 景德王 to Sinan 新安 (*SGSG*, 34, 7) and later to Pyŏkchin kun 碧珍郡. It has been a *kun* since 1895. *TYS*, 28, 17a–b.

11 This according to the Introduction to *HKC* by Ch'oe Nam-sŏn (p. 75). The Kwangmun hoe was organized in 1910 by Ch'oe with a view to preserving the Korean classics and disseminating them among scholars. The association published seventeen titles before 1945.

12 Introduction, pp. 1–6; chap. 1, pp. 7–21; chap. 2, pp. 22–30. Pak Pong-u 朴奉右, in his "Ch'ŏnggu sŭngjŏn poram" 靑丘僧傳寶覽, published in the *Shin pulgyo* 新佛敎, nos. 21–27 (February-November, 1940), incorporates practically all of *HKC*. Ch'oe Nam-sŏn, in his *Tonggyŏng t'ongji* 東京通志 (Kyŏngju, 1933), 2, 30b3–32a2, quotes the life of Pŏpkong without the eulogy. In May 1956 Tongguk University reprinted the *Dainihon bukkyō zensho* text as the first number in the *Changwoe chamnok* series, without any emendation or improvement.

13 There was a brief notice of the book by Imanishi Ryū in *SR* 史林, 3 (July 1918), 452–458 (reprinted in his *Kōraishi kenkyū* [Keijō, 1944], pp. 223–235). A brief description of the contents appeared in English in the *Asiatic Research [Center] Bulletin*, vol. 4, no. 9 (January 1962), 18–23.

14 For I-ching's biography see *SKSC* 1, *T*. 50, 710b–711a, and for his translations, *T*. 55, 567a–568b.

In compiling the *Lives*, Kakhun was working within a well-established tradition. He had at least three prototypes, not to mention a large body of historical and literary materials from China and Korea. The Korean sources he cites are documents and records of great antiquity, of which a few are still extant. Among the Chinese sources, he is most indebted for form and style to the three *Kao-seng chuan*, from which he seems to have adopted the subordinate biography, the *lun* 論, and the eulogy, the *ts'an* 贊.[15] There are, however, differences. The *lun*, which normally is found at the end of each category in Chinese biographical collections, comes only at the beginning, and the *ts'an* following the individual biography is composed not in verse but in ornate, allusion-packed prose. The *lun* (*non* in Korean) outlines the history of Buddhism in China and Korea from the time of its introduction to the thirteenth century. Here Kakhun, out of Buddhist piety, uncritically accepts the dates of the Buddha as 1027–949 B.C., as advocated by T'an-wu-tsui 曇無最.[16] Similar critical lapses can be found in the entries on Tamsi 曇始 and Hyŏnjo 玄照. In the first case, perhaps out of respect for his Chinese colleague, Kakhun copies almost verbatim the account of Tamsi (T'an-shih or Hui-shih 惠始) in the *Kao-seng chuan*, without fully understanding the nature and significance of the Buddhist persecution under the Northern Wei.[17] As for the famous T'ang pilgrim Hyŏnjo (Hsüan-chao),[18] we are simply told that he was a Silla national, without documentation.

Such minor lapses aside, Kakhun is a conscientious recorder of facts. Time and again he laments the paucity of materials. The ravages of time and havoc of wars were such that it is frightening to learn how little was preserved even in his own time. We glimpse Kakhun fighting desperately to shore up whatever remains there were of the civilization of the Three Kingdoms and Silla

---

15 Wright, "Hui-chiao's *Lives*," pp. 390–392, 407.

16 According to the theory advanced by him at the debate in 520 (*HKSC*, 23, 624c26–625a4, and *KHMC* 1, *T*. 52, 100c10), the Buddha entered Nirvāṇa in the *jen-shen* year of King Mu, for which see Yamanouchi Shinkyō 山內晉卿, *Shina bukkyōshi no kenkyū* 支那佛教史の研究 (Kyoto, 1921), pp. 162–165; Zürcher, I, 273; references in *HJAS*, 15 (1952), 188–189, n. 94; and Kenneth K. S. Ch'en, *Buddhism in China: A Historical Survey* (Princeton, 1964), pp. 29, 185.

17 The falsity of this account has been pointed out by Tsukamoto Zenryū 塚本善隆 in *Shina bukkyōshi kenkyū* (*Monumenta Serica*, 16 [1957], 370) and by Wright, "Hui-chiao's *Lives*," pp. 394–395, n. 5, and *HJAS*, 26 (1966), 307.

18 For his biography see Ch'en, *Buddhism in China*, pp. 234–235, and Paul Demiéville, *Le Concile de Lhasa* (Paris, 1952), pp. 185–186, n. 3.

periods. In the biography of the anonymous correspondent of Chih Tun
支遁,[19] he laments: "After the introduction of Buddhism into Korea from
Chin, there must have been heroic personages during the times of Sung and
Ch'i, but regrettably no record of them exists."[20] He registers his sorrow again
at the end of the same section: "What is really regrettable is that no good
historian kept a detailed record."[21] Concerning the unreliability of the sources
on Sundo 順道, either of Eastern Chin or of Former Ch'in,[22] Kakhun comments: "What a waste of the man and his excellences! For there should be
records on bamboo and silk glorifying his admirable accomplishment. Yet
only a [small] number of his writings remain; one wonders why this is so."[23]
For the historian the only solution is, as Kakhun declares in the biography
of Hyŏnyu 玄遊, that his contribution "be recorded in history and [thus]
shown to posterity."[24]

Kakhun, then, as a writer versed in Chinese historiography, was a trans-
mitter, not a creator; and he was quick to point out that his work was transmission.[25] He respected the materials at hand and was careful to cite his sources.
In cases involving reconstruction owing to the poor condition of the manuscript
or kindred materials, he clearly admits this, as in the biography of Anham:
"Ten logographs on the slab are eroded and four or five more are unclear.
The author takes what is legible and reconstructs the text by surmise."[26]
When he cannot supply the dates of his subjects he says so with disarming
frankness, as with the death date of Ŭiyŏn 義淵: "History does not relate
his end; I therefore leave it unmentioned."[27] Cases involving conflicting

---

19 For his biography see *KSC*, 4, 348b–349c. Also see Fukunaga Mitsuji 福永光司, "Shiton to
sono shūi," *Bukkyō shigaku* 佛教史學, 5 (March 1956), 12–34, and Paul Demiéville, "La pénétration
du Bouddhisme dans la tradition philosophique chinoise," *Cahiers d'Histoire Mondiale*, 3 (1956),
26–28.
20 *HKC*, 1016b2–4.
21 *HKC*, 1016b8–9.
22 Three locales are advanced as the place of origin of Sundo: (1) Former Ch'in (*SGSG*, 18, 3,
and *HKC*, 1016a7); (2) Eastern Chin (*HKC*, 1016a9–10); and (3) Wei (*SGYS*, 3, 121, where
Iryŏn quotes a certain biography of monks only to refute it).
23 *HKC*, 1016a18–20.
24 *HKC*, 1022c20.
25 Wright, "Hui-chiao's *Lives*," and Denis Twitchett, "Problems of Chinese Biography," in
Wright and Twitchett, eds., *Confucian Personalities* (Stanford, 1962), pp. 24–39.
26 *HKC*, 1022a18.
27 *HKC*, 1016c22–23.

information on a given topic offer him a chance to make an exhortation to posterity to do research, as with the two Buddhist names of Pŏpkong 法空: "Those who are interested in antiquity will do well to study the matter."[28] In yet another instance, after giving us no less than four theories[29] concerning the introduction of Buddhism into Silla, he adds, "What a discrepancy concerning the dates of Ado's life! Old records must be scrutinized carefully."[30]

Because Buddhism enjoyed seven centuries of uninterrupted prestige and protection as the state religion, Kakhun did not have to naturalize monks or to advance their status in Korean history.[31] What he wanted to do, however, was to prove that his subjects were on a par with their Chinese counterparts in every respect. For this purpose, he brings in Buddhist notables of the past and uses them figuratively, in ways that involve parallelism or imply contrast or superiority. Sundo, the first missionary to Koguryŏ, is termed a "peer of Dharmaratna 法蘭 and Seng-hui 僧會"[32] for his crusade in a foreign country and for his "great wisdom and wise counsel."[33] Wŏn'gwang 圓光, who used

---

28 *HKC*, 1019b11–12.

29 In chronological order they are: (1) Ado was an illegitimate son born to a Wei envoy, Kulma 崛摩, and a Koguryŏ woman, Ko To-nyŏng 高道寧. In 263 Ado went to Silla from Koguryŏ. This information is supposed to be contained in the *Sui chŏn* 殊異傳, according to *HKC* (*SGSG*, 4, 4; *SGYS*, 3, 122–123). The year 263 was obtained by counting 250 years (three thousand months in the prophecy uttered by Ado's mother) back from 527, the year Buddhism was allowed to be practiced in Silla. (2) During the time of King Nulchi 訥祇王 (417–458), Mukhoja 墨胡子 came from Koguryŏ (*SGYS*, 3, 122). (3) During the time of King Pich'ŏ 毗處王 (479–500), Ado, with three attendants, came to Morye's 毛禮 house. His appearance was strikingly similar to that of Mukhoja (*SGSG*, 4, 3). (4) Ado came to Ilsŏn kun 一善郡 on March 11, 527, according to the ancient records now lost.

The *Sisa* 詩史, quoted by *HKC*, offers essentially the same account, except that it places the origin of a Chinese envoy in Liang instead of Wei. Yi Ki-baek 李基白 thinks that (1) is out of the question because the state of Wei did not exist at that time, and proposes that we recognize two Ados, one who came to Koguryŏ and another who came to Silla. If Ado came to Koguryŏ, he was from the Former Ch'in rather than Eastern Chin (*Yŏksa hakpo* 歷史學報, 6 [1954], 134, n. 1, and 140–141). Yi opts for (3) because of the friendly relations that existed between Silla and Koguryŏ at that time (*ibid.*, 136–137, n. 1, and 138, n. 4). Eda Shunyū 江田俊雄, in *Bunka* 文化, 2 (1935), 968, feels that (2) is possible because King Pich'ŏ (or Soji 炤知) already kept a monk in his palace (*SGYS*, 4, 54–55) and because the king's predecessor had the Buddhist name *Chabi* ("compassion"). Suematsu Yasukazu 末松保和 takes (4) to be the most likely, in *Shiragi-shi no shomondai* 新羅史の諸問題 (Tokyo, 1954), pp. 212–216, 222.

30 *HKC*, 1018c25–26.

31 For the status and function of monks in Silla and other kingdoms see Yi Ki-baek, *yŏksa hakpo*, 6 (1954), 182–191.

32 *HKC*, 1016a23–24

33 *HKC*, 1016a22.

the *ko-i* 格義 method[34] in his exegesis of Buddhist doctrine, is rightly compared with Hui-yüan 慧遠 (334–416),[35] who used the same technique of *explication de texte* extensively two hundred years before. And the hardships suffered by five Silla pilgrims to China and India are compared with those of the envoys Chang Ch'ien 張騫[36] and Su Wu 蘇武.[37]

But equalization was not enough. To Kakhun's eye, some of his subjects were decidedly superior to their Chinese counterparts. Such is the case of Ado 阿道, the first missionary to Silla, who is praised for the prudence and judiciousness wherewith he "tried [his] plans first before carrying out the work of propagation."[38] The author's appraisal ends with more than a comparison: "Even Li-fang 利方 of Ch'in or [Kāśyapa] Mātaṇga 摩騰 of Han could not surpass [him]."[39] Again, as a parallel and contrast to Pŏpkong, who had renounced the throne to join the religious order, Emperor Wu of Liang is brought in only to be dismissed as a less-than-ideal monarch. Kakhun comments: "It is... wrong to compare him [Pŏpkong] with [Emperor] Wu of Liang, for while the latter served in the T'ung-t'ai monastery as a servant and let his imperial work fall to the ground, the former first surrendered his throne in order to install his heir and only afterwards became a monk."[40] Pŏpkong is an ideal ruler, argues Kakhun, for his Buddhist fervor brought about not the downfall but rather the consolidation and prosperity of the kingdom.

True, the age of Buddhism in Korea began with Pŏpkong. But this would

34 For *Ko-i* see T'ang Yung-t'ung, "On Ko-yi, the Earliest Method by which Indian Buddhism and Chinese Thought Were synthesized," in *Radhakrishnan: Comparative Studies in Philosophy* (London, 1951), pp. 276–286.

35 For Hui-yüan, Tao-an's disciple and founder of the "White Lotus Community" on Mount Lu in 402, see *KSC*, 6, 357c–361b. For his ko-i method see Demiéville, *Cahiers d'Histoire Mondiale*, 3 (1956), 23–24. For more on Hui-yüan see bibliography in Ch'en, *Buddhism in China*, pp. 515–516, See also n. 413 to the translation.

36 *Shih chi*, 123, 0267a–b (Watson, *Records of the Grand Historian of China*, II, 267–274, *passim*); *Ch'ien Han shu*, 61, 0509c–0510c; 95, 0603b; Frederick Hirth, "The Story of Chang Ch'ien, China's Pioneer in West Asia," *JAOS*, 37 (1917), 89–152; Joseph Needham, *Science and Civilization in China* (Cambridge, 1954), I, 107–108; and Kuwabara Jitsuzō 桑原隲藏, "Chō Ken no ensei," *Tōzai kōtsūshi ronsō* 東西交通史論叢 (Tokyo, 1944), pp. 1–117.

37 For Su Wu, who returned to China in 81 B.C. after nineteen years of captivity by the Huns, see *Shih chi*, 110, 0247a (Watson, *Records of the Grand Historian of China*. II, 190); *Ch'ien Han shu*, 7,0308b (Homer H. Dubs, *The History of the Former Han Dynasty*, II [Baltimore, 1954], 161).

38 *HKC*, 1018b4.

39 *HKC*, 1018b5–6.

40 *HKC*, 1019b18–20.

not have been possible unless Silla had been a land chosen and blessed by the former Buddha and unless former kings had accumulated meritorious karma from the beginning of the country's history. Thus arose, from about the beginning of the sixth century, a belief that Korea was the land of the former Buddha. Such a belief is present in several episodes in the *Lives*. The first time we encounter it is in the biography of Ado, where Ado's mother, before dispatching him to the barbarous country of Silla to propagate the faith, remarks: "Although at this moment there is no oral transmission of the doctrine in that land of Silla, three thousand months from now an enlightened king, a protector of the Law, shall hold sway and greatly advance the Buddha's cause. In the capital, there are seven places where the Law shall abide. . . . At these places are ruins of monasteries *(saṅghārāma)* built during the time of the former Buddha, which escaped earlier destruction."[41] There were such remains, according to the *Lives*, in the Forest of the Heavenly Mirror 天鏡林 in the year 534 when trees were felled in order to build a monastery.[42] "When the ground was cleared, pillar bases, stone niches, and steps were discovered, proving the site to be that of an old monastery *(cāturdiśa)*."[43] When the Great Master Wŏn'gwang, shortly after his return from Sui in 600, went to inspect a site where a monastery was to be built, he found the remains of a stone pagoda,[44] again indicating the site of a former monastery. Still another site mentioned is that east of Wŏlsŏng 月城 and south of the Dragon Palace 龍宮, where the Hwangnyong monastery 皇龍寺 was built and where, according to the *Samguk yusa*, a stone was found upon which Kāśyapa and Śākyamuni used to sit in meditation.[45] There was, too, a brisk traffic between Korea and India. The gold that Great King Aśoka shipped to Sap'o 絲浦 was used in 574 to cast a Buddhist image, sixteen feet high, at the Hwangnyong monastery.[46] Although Kakhun is quick to point out that this lore represents nothing more than tradition, all of it was pretty much part of the common belief of the time in which he must have felt a secret joy and pride.

---

41 *HKC*, 1018b3–9.
42 This was the Hŭngnyun monastery, for which see nn. 234 and 280 to the translation.
43 *HKC*, 1019a26–27.
44 *HKC*, 1021a6.
45 *SGYS*, 3, 132, 137.
46 *HKC*, 1019c5–7.

As befitted the rulers of the land of the former Buddha, the Silla kings were said to be of the Kṣatriya caste. This revelation was, according to Iryŏn, made by Mañjuśrī himself when he appeared in the form of an old man to the Vinaya master Chajang 慈藏[47] on Mount Wu-t'ai 五臺山.[48] The Bodhisattva addressed the Silla pilgrim: "Your sovereign is of the Kṣatriya caste [of India, which is] far different from other barbarian tribes in the East."[49] When Mañjuśrī appeared again in the form of an old monk, he advised the master Chajang to return to his country and visit Mount Odae 五臺山,[50] where ten thousand Mañjuśrī reside always.[51] With this episode,

---

[47] His surname was Kim, his given name Sŏnjong 善宗; he was born on the Buddha's birthday. He went to T'ang in 636 (or 638, according to *HKSC*, 24, 639b13) with his disciple Sil 實 and others. He went first to Mount Wu-t'ai to worship Mañjuśrī, then to Ch'ang-an, and finally to the Yün-che monastery 雲際寺 on Mount Chung-nan to study. At the request of Queen Sŏndŏk he returned in 643 with 400 cases of Buddhist scriptures (*SGSG*, 5, 3). He built the T'ongdo monastery 通度寺 (*CJS*, I, 532–534) in Yangsan and established the Vinaya school in Korea. He lectured chiefly on the *Mahāyānasaṃgraha* and the latter part of the *Brahmajāla*. For his biography see *HKSC*, 24, 639a8–640a2; *SGYS*, 4, 191–194; and *Tongsa yŏlchŏn* 東師列傳 (*Changwoe chamnok*, II [1957], 5–8). Scattered references to him also occur in *SGYS*, 1, 69; 3, 137–140, 165–170, 171–172. The relics in the T'ongdo monastery that Chajang brought over from China were moved by Sejong to the Buddha Hall in the palace, but were finally returned to China when Huang Yen came to Korea (1419) to collect sacred objects. They were offered to Ming as part of the 558 pieces that Huang carried away (*Sejong sillok* 世宗實錄, 5, 8b; 16a).

[48] For Wu-t'ai (or Ch'ing-liang, Śīta or Śīsīra?), see *TP*, 48 (1960), 54–61, and Demiéville, *Le Concile de Lhasa*, pp. 376–377. According to *SGYS*, 3, 165–166, the sole purpose of Chajang's trip to China was to witness Mañjuśrī on Wu-t'ai. Perhaps, like most Chinese and Korean devotees, he believed that the *Avataṃsaka* was preached by Śākyamuni and collated by Mañjuśrī. Tao-hsüan 道宣, however, does not record the pilgrimage in his biography of Chajang. Iryŏn's explanation is that Chajang kept it secret during his stay in China (*SGYS*, 4, 192). Ennin 圓仁, who himself made a pilgrimage to Wu-t'ai during his stay in China (838–847), reports a similar story related to Buddhapāla that he heard there. See his *Nittō guhō junrei kōki* 入唐求法巡禮行記 (*Dainihon bukkyō zensho*, 113; Tokyo,1918), 3, 237b–238a (Edwin O. Reischauer, *Ennin's Diary* [New York, 1955], pp. 246–247); 3, 243b (Reischauer, p. 266).

[49] *SGYS*, 3, 137–138. This must be one of the reasons why Silla kings, aside from their Buddhist piety and fervor, adopted Buddhist names. The title of the twentieth king of Silla was Chabi; that of the twenty-third king, Pŏphŭng; the tabu-name of the twenty-fourth king was Sammaekchong 三麥宗 or Simmaekpu 深麥夫, which is considered to be a transcription of *śramaṇa;* that of the twenty-sixth king, Chinp'yŏng 眞平 (579–632), Śuddhodana, and of his queen, Māyā, and finally that of Queen Chindŏk, Śrīmālā. See Yi Ki-baek, *Yŏksa hakpo*, 6 (1954), 189, n. 21.

[50] Upon his return to Silla in 643, Chajang immediately climbed Mount Odae (*TYS*, 44, 5b) for a vision of Mañjuśrī, but owing to the darkness that lasted for three days he was unable to witness the Bodhisattva. He returned then to the Wŏnnyŏng monastery 元寧寺 and finally saw Mañjuśrī. He then moved to the Chŏngam monastery 淨嵒寺, which after his death was repaired by the monk Yuyŏn 有緣 and called the Wŏlchŏng 月精寺 (*SGYS*, 3, 166, and *CJS*, II, 33–35; but *TYS*, 44, 18b, reports that the Wŏlchŏng was erected by Chajang). In 705 King Sŏngdŏk 聖德王 (702–737)

Silla became at once not only the land of the former Buddha but the land of the present and future Buddha as well, in other words, the permanent abode of the Buddha and the Bodhisattvas.

The myths and legends engendered by Buddhist piety in fact seem to determine the very nature of Buddhist biography. That is, the world this kind of writing refers to is a world presided over by the Buddha with his universal Law, by miraculous wonders and wondrous miracles, and by the relentless workings of karmic rewards and retributions. Indeed, this referential world hitherto unknown to the Koreans, was a world unto itself, one with a concept of time and space all its own. Subjects of the *Lives*, or, for that matter, subjects of any *Kao-seng chuan*, therefore move in a world where they sense the hand of the Buddha working at every moment and in every corner.[52] Not until their maturity do most of them make their appearance in history. No striking details are given about their characters or personalities; these must be inferred from stock phrases which suggest their behavior patterns. Some were already blessed with enlightenment at birth (Anham),[53] or were self-enlightened (Āryavarman);[54] but even less fortunate ones possessed "profound understanding and broad learning" (Ŭiyŏn),[55] "unfathomable holiness" (Kaktŏk),[56] "extraordinary understanding" (Wŏn'gwang),[57] "great wisdom and insight" (Hyŏn'gak),[58] or an "otherworldly, harmonious nature" (Hyŏnyu).[59] Less favored ones still, like Sundo, at least "vigorously practiced virtue" and were "compassionate and patient in helping living beings."[60]

---

erected a hall for Mañjuśrī, had his image enshrined, and had monks copy the *Avataṁsaka* (*SGYS*, 3, 168). For more legends centering around this sacred mountain in Korea see *SGYS*, 3, 170–171.

51 I follow *SGYS*, 3, 166, which reads: 一萬文殊常住在彼. Compare the reading in *T*. 9, 590a3–5, which differs: . . . 彼現有菩薩名文殊師利, 有一萬菩薩眷屬常受說法. See also *Bunka*, 2 (1935), 985–988, and 21 (1957), 562–573.

52 For a comparison with Western hagiography see Paul Murray Kendall, *The Art of Biography* (New York, 1965), pp. 40 ff., 106; Helen C. White, *Tudor Books of Saints and Martyrs* (Madison, 1963), pp. 4–30; and James L. Clifford, ed., *Biography as an Art* (New York, 1962), p. x.

53 *HKC*, 1021c7–8.

54 *HKC*, 1022a25.

55 *HKC*, 1016b17.

56 *HKC*, 1020a17.

57 *HKC*, 1020c2–3.

58 *HKC*, 1022b27.

59 *HKC*, 1022c9.

60 *HKC*, 1016a4.

By the time we come to Hyŏnt'ae 玄太, we cannot but feel that the compiler's imagination has failed him or that he was too tired to pull out yet another index card from his file, for we are told only that Hyŏnt'ae was "pensive as a child, and [that] he had the marks *(lakṣaṇa)* of a great man *(Mahāpuruṣa)."*[61]

Since extraordinary potentialities are present in all of them from birth, their future successes are easy to prognosticate. Some of them perform miracles (Tamsi, Ado, Anham), cure incurable illness (Wŏn'gwang, Ado), or communicate with supernatural beings such as spirits, dragons, and heavenly messengers (Wŏn'gwang, Mālānanda). Miracles also accompany their activities. Both Heaven and Earth tremble in announcing the advent of Ado, and wondrous flowers rain from Heaven during his sermon; music fills the air and unusual fragrance is noticed at the death of Wŏn'gwang. After death one monk, Anham, is seen riding squarely on the green waves, joyfully heading west. Often we are told of the subjects' feats of endurance against fire, wild beast, or sword and axe, experiences from which, having mastered the elements of nature, they always emerge intact. But should they suffer death, permitted by the Buddha to glorify his religion, miracles of the most spectacular nature take place, as in the case of the martyrdom of Ich'adon 異次頓.[62]

Finally, the compiler's attempt to give color or luster to his subjects results in the repetition of conventional epithets. Ŭiyŏn is "a leader of both monks and laymen,"[63] "a ferry on the sea of suffering,"[64] or the "middle beam over the gate of the Law."[65] Chimyŏng's moral power is "as high as Mount Sung 嵩

---

61 *HKC*, 1022c24.

62 For Ich'adon see n. 263 to the translation. Concerning the magic and miracles of eminent monks Murakami Yoshimi has an interesting article in *Tōhō shūkyō*, 17 (1961), 1–17. After a study of theurgists in chapters 9 and 10 of *KSC*, he suggests: (1) Magic practiced by Buddhist missionaries was a means to an end, but being motivated by compassion, it had the power of salvation; (2) these monks had to attach themselves to the non-Chinese rulers in the North in order to gain their confidence and support for propagation, but their ultimate goal was the salvation of the people; (3) their magic is related to the *abhijñā;* (4) the occultism in Hsien Taoism (*JAOS*, 76 [1956], 143) owes a great deal to theurgy imported from the Western Regions; (5) there is an element of Hsien Taoism in Buddhist magic, suggesting a fusion of Buddhism and Hsien Taoism. Although theurgy is in the line of magic and fetish, in the Six Dynasties period it had a philosophical and religious background to support it; hence a future study should investigate its relationship to contemporary learning and culture. For theurgy in the Neoplatonic school see E. R. Dodds, *The Greeks and the Irrational* (Berkeley and Los Angeles, 1951), pp. 283–311.

63 *HKC*, 1016b18.

64 *HKC*, 1016c19.

65 *HKC*, 1016c19–20.

or Mount Hua 華," his magnanimity "as deep as a wide ocean."[66] A single epithet, "a lotus in the fire," singles out Hyŏn'gak from the others.[67] Rarely is animal imagery used; a "lion" roaming alone in the wilderness[68] occurs, fittingly, in allusion to the pilgrim Hyŏnt'ae as he braves the hardships of crossing the Himālayas, but such an instance of creative imagination is exceptional.

After plowing through the *Lives,* one wonders whether the stock phrases and behavior patterns used would satisfy even the most modest demands of twentieth-century curiosity. Such archetypal themes of life as hope and fear, pride and prejudice, struggle and triumph are present. Often there are descriptions of the hardships and obstacles that the monks have had to overcome in order to fulfill their mission, such as the taunts of the enemy, the ignorance of masses, the tyranny of the ruler, or the impassability of nature. There are also moving accounts of experiences endured and sacrifices made for the propagation and glory of the religion. But upon scrutiny these monks evaporate into the vast realm of the Dharma. From the beginning, they are placed on a plane high above ordinary people, where their suffering and struggling are only precious memories, "glittering exempla for the future believers."[69] What the compiler emphasizes is precisely what sets them apart from ordinary people: their aloofness from human weakness and frailty. Indeed, they are, as Kakhun states, "as remote from us as the easternmost extremity,"[70] and writing of their lives is as difficult as "catching the wind or grasping a reflection."[71]

True, there is a span of from nearly six hundred to a thousand years separating Kakhun from his subjects. The more remote in time a subject is, the more remote he becomes as an individual. There are, too, insurmountable gaps. One seldom discerns any attempt to place the subject in the diurnal course of existence. Prenatal wonders, amazing precocity, feats of endurance, wonderworking and miracles—these familiar formulae and patterns are the very stuff from which the compiler worked up his accounts. Indeed, such a common

---

66 *HKC,* 1020b21.
67 *HKC,* 1022b28.
68 *HKC,* 1022c27.
69 White, *Tudor Books of Saints and Martyrs,* p. 17.
70 *HKC,* 1023a3.
71 *HKC,* 1018c3.

stock of references has supplied the deficiency in both knowledge and style of many of the biographies.[72] But for Kakhun's readers it was this very repetition of formulaic detail which drove home the existence of the spiritual world of the Buddha and proved its endless workings through the medium of the eminent monks. The reality of the Dharma and karma, otherwise not apparent to mundane eyes, was thus made manifest to believers and nonbelievers alike.

After scrutinizing the *Lives* with respect to its historical context, referential world, techniques, and behavior patterns, I am compelled to conclude that it is, if anything, what Paul Murray Kendall calls "demand biography," that is, "biography produced to satisfy the requirements or the predilections of an age, to act as a beast of burden for ends other than the illumination of life."[73] The purpose of the *Lives* is edification. It is an instrument for conversion and the propagation of the faith. It is propaganda because it persuasively purveys a specific doctrine and upholds the values of eminent monks as a model for emulation. As the theme in Western hagiography from A.D. 400 to 1400 was the glory of God through the praise of His saints, so the theme in the *Lives* is the glory of the world of the Dharma through the lives of its monks. Such generalized biography is hardly life-writing in the truest sense of the word. It does not illuminate or recreate man but deforms him into a simulacrum of life, an exemplum of the wonderful world of the Law.[74] But these faults are not entirely the compiler's. The limits of the *Lives* are the limits imposed by the view of man that prevailed at that time; they are determined by the social and cultural forces at work.

The secular and nationalistic aspects of Silla Buddhism are best exemplified in the master Wŏn'gwang's "Five Commandments for Laymen" and in the institution of the *hwarang*, an indigenous system whereby aristocratic youth were recruited to fill key political and military roles during Silla's period of nation-building. The five commandments deal with such virtues as loyalty, filial piety, sincerity, courage, and goodness (benevolence). But what is remarkable is the master's ability to meet the current situation and to adapt his teaching to the demands of the occasion. Silla was then in a national crisis, and its survival depended on the undivided loyalty and service of the people.

---

72 White, *Tudor Books of Saints and Martyrs*, p. 17.

73 Kendall, *Art of Biography*, pp. 40–41.

74 *Ibid.*, p. 104.

Two youths who received the master's instruction carried his precepts into practice in 602 by dying in action in a battle against Paekche. A guiding spirit in the cultivation of the *hwarang* was also provided by eminent monks. They not only counseled the members of the *hwarang* as to conduct in the light of the "Five Commandments" but served them as chaplains in their liberal education and perhaps even on the battlefield.[75] Scattered references in historical sources suggest that some members of the *hwarang* were believed to be reincarnations of Maitreya;[76] and Kim Yu-sin, a leader of the *hwarang*, and his group were called the *Yonghwa hyangdo*[77] 龍華香徒, a "band of the Dragon Flower tree," the bodhi tree of Maitreya when he comes to earth to save the living beings. What sustained the *hwarang* was this belief in Maitreya, a patron saint of the institution, and the belief that its members were no less than reincarnated Maitreyas.[78] Indeed, Buddhism provided a formidable ideology for the unification and protection of the country.

Yet the ultimate function of the *Lives* is more secular than one is led to believe. From the time of its introduction, Buddhism in Korea was closely related to the state and the ruling house.[79] The king enforced the *vinaya* and

75 Silla monks Pŏpchang 法藏 and Hyein 慧忍 accompanied King Chinhŭng (534–576) on his tours of inspection of the country (*CKS*, I, 9; *SG*, 2 [1930], 85). Kŏch'ilpu was a commander in a battle against Koguryŏ along the Han (*SGSG*, 44, 2–3). Monks performed similar duties in Koguryŏ and Paekche. The monk Torim 道琳 was a successful spy in Paekche (*SGSG*, 25, 7–8); and the monk Toch'im 道琛 (d. 661) plotted a revival of Paekche after its fall (*SGSG*, 28, 5–6). See *Yŏksa hakpo*, 6 (1954), 182.

76 Chinja 眞慈 (or Chŏngja 貞慈) of the Hŭngnyun monastery prayed to Maitreya that he appear in Silla in the form of a *hwarang* (*SGYS*, 3, 153–155; *Pulgyo hakpo* 佛教學報, 3–4 [1966], 135–149); and Knight Chukchi 竹旨郎 (or Chungman 竹曼) was thought to be a reincrnation of Maitreya (*SGYS*, 2, 77–78). For a discussion of how the extant Buddhist sculpture mirrors this trend, both official and popular, in Silla Buddhism, see Chewon Kim and Won-yong Kim, *Treasures of Korean Art* (New York, 1966), pp. 119 ff.

77 *SGSG*, 41, 2.

78 Yaotani Takayasu, 八百谷孝保 in *Shichō* 史潮, 7 (1937), 649–656.

79 See *Yŏksa hakpo*, 6 (1954), 146 ff. Some Silla monarchs might have compared themselves to a Bodhisattva Cakravartin, but seldom to a Tathāgata. It is a commonplace to say that during the Nan-pei ch'ao the emperor was considered in the North to be a Tathāgata and in the South a Bodhisattva. In an article in the *Bukkyō shigaku*, 10 (March 1962), 1–15, Suzuki Keizō 鈴木啓造 submits this equation to a fresh valuation. He cites a few instances concerning the North. For instance, Wei Shou's *Shih-lao chih* 釋老志 quotes a saying attributed to Fa-kuo in which he compared Emperor Tao-wu (371–386–409) of Wei to a Tathāgata (Hurvitz, p. 53; Ch'en, *Buddhism in China*, p. 146). Also, Wei Yüan-sung 衞元嵩 (*HKSC*, 35, 657c–658c), in a memorial presented to the Emperor Wu of the Northern Chou (543–561–577–578), likens the emperor to a Tathāgata. The same source also quotes the conversation held in 577 between Jen Tao-lin 任道林 and the emperor in which the latter

protected the *sangha,* and the *sangha* in turn prayed for the country and helped the administration to implement its policies.[80] This close interrelationship is well illustrated by the popularity of the *Suvarṇaprabāsa* 金光明經[81] and *Jen-wang ching* 仁王經.[82] In the former, the four deva kings pledge themselves to protect a ruler who reads and worships the *sūtra*;[83] in the latter, the same pledge is made by the World-Honored One himself.[84] In order, therefore, to protect and encourage the Dharma and to receive the promised blessings, a number of treatises were written on these sūtras[85] and the Assemblies of Benevolent Kings 仁王會[86] were held to read and elucidate them. The initia-

suggests such an equation, only to be discouraged by the former. Indeed, some might have wished to believe in such an equation, but, as Suzuki argues, Emperor Wu's view was not endorsed by the clergy. It is true that the emperors who were likened either to a Bodhisattva or a Tathāgata were all protectors of Buddhism. But it is difficult to accept this as a characteristic of Buddhism either in the South or in the North. For instances of the emperor-Bodhisattva equation see *KHMC*, 4, *T.* 52, 112b–20–21; 28, *T.* 52, 330a1 and 326a15; and *HKSC*, 25, 650b9–11.

80 See, for instance, Kim Tong-hwa (2), 31–41; for a general discussion centering on Chinese Buddhism see Ōchō Enichi, *Chūgoku bukkyō no kenkyū* (Kyoto, 1958), pp. 326–381; Wing-tsit Chan, "Transformation of Buddhism in China," *Philosophy East and West,* 7 (1958), 107–116.

81 Three Chinese translations are extant: (1) by Dharmarakṣa, between 412 and 421, in 4 chapters (*T.* 16, 335a–359b); (2) by Pao-kuei, Yen-tsung, et al., in 8 chapters (*T.* 16, 359b–402a); and (3) by I-ching, in 703, in 10 chapters (*T.* 16, 403a–456c [trans. Johannes Nobel, *Suvarṇaprabhāsottama-sūtra,* 2 vols., Leiden, 1958]). For a description of the contents see M. W. de Visser, *Ancient Buddhism in Japan* (Leiden, 1935), I, 263–269, 431 ff. For its reception in China and Japan see Kanaoka Shūyū 金岡秀友, "Kongōmyōkyō no teiōkan to sono Shina-Nihonteki juyō," *Bukkyō shigaku,* 6 (1957), 267–278.

82 The sūtra was translated by Dharmapāla; by Kumārajīva (*KT.* 5, 1021a–1033c; *T.* 8, 825a–834a); by Paramārtha; and by Amoghavajra (*T.* 8, 834a–835a). Among the four new commentaries, a noteworthy one is that by a Silla monk, Wŏnch'ŭk 圓測 (613–696), in 6 chapters (*T.* 33, 359a–427c; *Zokuzōkyō* IA, 40/3–4, 284c–363a). See Edward Conze, *The Prajñāpāramitā Literature* (The Hague, 1960), pp. 18, 29, 76–77.

83 *T.* 16, 427c6 ff. (Nobel, *Suvarṇaprabhāsottama-sūtra,* I, 192 ff.).

84 *T.* 8, 829c–830a, 840a.

85 Wŏnch'ŭk (*T.* 55, 1170b24; *BKD,* VIII, 386d–387c) and Taehyŏn 大賢 (*T.* 55, 1170b 26) commented on the *Jen-wang ching,* and Wŏnhyo 元曉 (*T.* 55, 1170b2), Taehyŏn (*T.* 55, 1170b8), and Kyŏnghŭng 憬興 (*T.* 55, 1170b7, and *BKD,* III, 435c, 437a) on the *Suvarṇaprabāsa.* See Cho Myŏng-gi 趙明基, *Silla pulgyo ŭi inyŏm kwa yŏksa* (1962), pp. 98, 166, 191, 213.

86 The first Assembly of One Hundred Seats 百座會 in Silla was held in 551 under the supervision of the Chief of Clerics, Hyeryang 惠亮 (*SGSG,* 44, 3). In the second recorded meeting, held in 613, the master Wŏn'gwang lectured on the scriptures. Altogether, eight such meetings were recorded after 613: to pray for the king's recovery from illness in 636 (*SGSG,* 5, 2) and 886 (*SGSG,* 11, 8); to pray for the repose of the deceased king during the time of King Sŏngdŏk (*SGYS,* 2, 78) and for the dead killed by an earthquake in 779 (*SGSG,* 9, 7); to lecture on the *Jen-wang ching* and pray for the peace and prosperity of the country in 876 (*SGSG,* 11, 6) and, twice, in 887 (*SGSG,* 11, 8); and in 924, when the king granted a maigre feast for 300 Dhyāna monks (*SGYS,* 2, 91). The first such

tion of the *P'algwanhoe* 八關會 in Silla also had as its function the protection of the country. The *p'algwanhoe* is a Buddhist ceremony in which the layman receives the eight prohibitory commands, which he vows to keep for one day and one night. The first mention of this ceremony in Silla occurs in 551[87] and the second on November 10,572.[88] In 636, by the shores of T'ai-hua lake 太華池[89] on Mount Wu-t'ai, the master Chajang met a deity who asked him to construct a nine-story pagoda[90] upon his return to Silla and to initiate the *p'algwanhoe* as the best means of protecting the country from invasions.[91] Although history does not mention the ceremony for the next three hundred years, until the beginning of Koryŏ, during the Koryŏ period the ceremony was codified and secularized and took place frequently, especially during such times of national crisis as the Khitan and Mongol invasions.[92]

The compilation of the *Lives*, like any other act of piety, was intended to "make the country and Buddhism prosper,"[93] as the compiler declares with vigorous conviction. Ich'adon, whose martyrdom heralded the Buddhist era in Silla, exclaims: "If we practice Buddhism, the whole country will become prosperous and peaceful."[94] Buddhism, Kakhun reminds us, is the only path able to ensure the efficacy of "the Deathless Medicine of the Law."[95]

What is, then, the nature of the *Lives* in the most comprehensive sense? It is a curious amalgam of religion, philosophy, history, and perhaps literature.[96] It is a complex organization of materials drawn from all the known

---

meeting in Koryŏ was held in 1012 (*KRS*, 4, 12a). The ceremony was firmly codified during the time of King Munjong (1019–1047–1082–1083), when regular meetings were held triennially, lasting usually for three days, with a granting of meal to 30,000 monks. In addition, unscheduled emergency meetings were convened, chiefly on occasions of natonal crisis or natural catastrophe. The last meeting of Koryŏ was held in the fourth month of 1373 (*KRS*, 44, 3a). See Ninomiya Keinin 二宮啓任, "Chōsen ni okeru Ninnōe no kaisetsu," *CG*, 14 (1959), 155–163.

87 *SGSG*, 44, 3.
88 *SGSG*, 4, 7.
89 T'ai-ho 太和 in *SGYS*, 3, 138 (*TP*, 48 [1960], 57).
90 Built in 645 (*SGSG*, 5, 4). See also *SGYS*, 3, 137–139.
91 *SGYS*, 3, 138.
92 For more on this, see n. 303 to the translation.
93 *HKC*, 1016b13.
94 *HKC*, 1019a6.
95 *T*. 8, 844c21–22.
96 That Kakhun was a superb stylist in Chinese, especially parallel prose, is evident throughout the *Lives*. The *non* can be cited as an example. Even if he drew on existing materials, he always

philosophies and ideologies of the time,[97] with multiple meanings and functions. Highly eclectic and syncretic in nature, it came into being to satisfy the wishes and needs of a particular audience in a particular time which espoused a particular brand of Buddhism. The curious nature and unusual function of the *Lives* are the very reasons for its existence, because, as T. S. Eliot remarks, "Nothing in this world or the next is a substitute for anything else."[98] Indeed, Kakhun successfully and pre-eminently performed what a Buddhist biographer would set out to do.

---

supplemented them, as in the case of Wŏn'gwang, with new materials written in a balanced, allusion-packed prose.

[97] Mishina Shōei 三品彰英 has noted certain similarities between the birth stories of Hyŏkkŏse 赫居世 and Puru 扶婁 and the stories about the origins of certain monasteries and famous Buddha images. He implies that the stories connected with culture heroes or foundation myths were, with minor changes, applied to the *pourquoi* stories of monasteries and statues. See his "Chōsen ni okeru bukkyō to minzoku shinkō," *Bukkyō shigaku,* 4 (1954), 18–21.

[98] *The Use of Poetry and the Use of Criticism* (Cambridge, Mass., 1933), p. 106.

LIVES OF EMINENT
KOREAN MONKS

The *non* 論[1] says the teaching of Buddha[2] is everlasting in its nature and function[3] and vast and deep in its vow of compassion *(karuṇa-praṇidhāna)*. [1015b] It exhaustively fulfills the Three Divisions of time *(tryadhvan)*[4] and embraces the Ten Directions;[5] it is nourished by rain and dew[6] and aroused by thunder and lightning.[7] It reaches its goal without walking, hurries without haste.[8] The Five Visions *(pañca-cakṣus)*[9] cannot discern its appearance; the Four Special Branches of Knowledge *(catasraḥ pratisaṃ-vidaḥ)*[10] cannot describe its form. Its substance is without coming or going, yet it functions with the display of coming and going.[11]

---

1 For Hui-chiao's definition of *lun* ("critical estimate") see *KSC*, 14, 419a, and Arthur F. Wright, "Hui-chiao's *Lives of Eminent Monks*," in *Silver Jubilee Volume of Zinbun Kagaku Kenkyūjo* (Kyoto, 1954), pp. 391 and 407.

2 For 佛陀 see, for example, Mou tzu's 牟子 definition in *T.* 52, 2a7–13 (Pelliot [6], 292); Fukui Kōjun's in *Tōyō shisōshi kenkyū* 東洋思想史研究 (Tokyo, 1960), pp. 170–186, which states that 佛 (**b'iwət*) has the same meaning as 彿 (**p'i̯wət*); and *T.* 25, 73a ff. (Lamotte, I, 137 ff.). For the possible etymology of the Korean word for Buddha, *puch'ŏ*, see Chŏng Yag-yong 丁若鏞, *Aŏn kakpi* 疋言覺非, in *Chŏng Tasan chŏnsŏ* 丁茶山全書 (3 vols.; 1960–1961), 1, 32a-b.

3 性相: the nature of anything and its phenomenal expression, 性 being nonfunctional, or noumenal, and 相, functional or phenomenal (*SH*, 259b).

4 三際: past, present, and future.

5 North, east, southwest, northeast, southeast, northwest, south, west, above, and below.

6 An allusion to 潤之以風雨 in *Chou i* 周易 *(SPTK)*, 7, 1a (Richard Wilhelm, *The I Ching or Book of Changes* [2 vols; New York., 1950], I, 306). Cf. *Mencius*, IVA, 8 (Legge, II, 407).

7 雷霆以鼓之: *Chou i*, 7, 1a (Wilhelm, I, 306).

8 A quotation from *Chou i*, 7, 9b 不疾而速 不行而至, but in reverse order (Wilhelm, I, 339).

9 The five superior qualities of vision, partly physical, partly mental or spiritual, possessed by a Buddha: bodily, divine, wisdom, doctrine, Buddha's eye (*BHSD*, p. 221b).

10 四辯 [四無礙解, 四解, 四智] *catasraḥ pratisaṃvidaḥ*, Four Discriminations or Special Branches of Knowledge: *dharma-, artha-, nirukti-*, and *pratibhāna-pratisaṃvid*. See *BHSD*, p. 370b, and *MBD*, III, 2020a–2021a.

11 *T'i* 體 has been rendered as "substance," and *yung* 用 as "functions with the display of." For

On the eighth day of the fourth month of the year *chia-yin* 甲寅 (1027 B.C.)[12] of King Chao, of Chou 周昭王 (1111–256 B.C.), Śākya Tathāgata entered the womb of Māyā, riding on the Candana Tower[13] 栴檀樓閣 from Tuṣita Heaven, and was born from the Māyā's right side, in the palace of King Śuddhodana.[14] That night, an emanation of five colors cut across the *T'ai-wei* 太微[15] constellation, illuminating the West. King Chao asked the Grand Astrologer Su Yu 蘇由 for the reason, and the latter answered, "A great sage is born in the West." [When the king] asked about the effect of this birth, Su Yu remarked, "There is no reason other than the following: his teaching will reach our land one thousand years hence."[16]

[Śākyamuni] at first lived in the palace as no more than a worldly person. On the eighth day of the fourth month of the year *chia-shen* 甲申 (997 B.C.),[17] when he was thirty,[18] he left home and went out of the city. He then sat under

---

these terms see Wing-tsit Chan, *A Source Book in Chinese Philosophy* (Princeton, 1963), p. 791; Kenneth K. S. Ch'en, *Buddhism in China: A Historical Survey* (Princeton, 1964), p. 87; *HJAS*, 10 (1947), 143 ff.; and *JAOS*, 85 (1965), 451.

12   1027 B.C. according to Tung Tso-pin, *Chronological Tables of Chinese History* (Hong Kong, 1960); 958 B.C. according to the *Chu-shu chi-nien* 竹書紀年 (*SPPY*). See Zürcher, I, 273–276. The date of his birth varies: April-May 558 B.C. (Louis Renou and Jean Filliozat, *L'Inde Classique*, II [Hanoi and Paris, 1953], 463 ff.; 543 B.C. (in Theravāda countries); 468 B.C. (Étienne Lamotte, *Histoire du Bouddhisme Indien, des Origines a l'ère Śaka* [Louvain, 1958], pp. 13–15); and 483 B.C. (*Cambridge History of India*, I [1922], 171). In Korea, however, either from miscalculation or a copyist's error, the dates of the Buddha's birth and death are not uniform in the sources. At least two different dates are given for his birth: 1027 B.C. (*CJS*, I, 105; II, 274, 392) and 1024 B.C. (*CKS*, I, 263). For his death there are at least four: 960 B.C. (*CKS*, I, 54), 950 B.C. (*TG*, 41, 364), 949 B.C. (*HKC*; *SGYS*, 3, 133; *CJS*, I, 263), and 941 B.C. (*TG*, 41, 365). For this see Fujita Ryōsaku 藤田亮策, "Chōsen no nengō to kinen," *TG*, 41 (1958), 364–366.

13   *MBD*, III, 2986c-2987c; Zürcher, II, 389, n. 44; *JA*, 236 (1948), 111, n. 1.

14   Father of Śākyamuni, king of Kapilavastu. For this and other matters related to Śākyamuni's chronology see *T*. 49, 142c-143a; Hayashiya Tomojirō, *Bukkyō oyobi bukkyōshi no kenkyū* (Tokyo, 1948), pp. 3–92; and Yamanouchi Shinkyō, *Shina bukkyōshi no kenkyū* (Kyoto, 1921), pp. 155–166.

15   The T'ai-wei-yüan is a sort of rough circle of ten stars in Virgo and Leo. The constellation T'ai-wei is just north of the celestial equator to the north of Chen-hsiu and I-hsiu, i.e., the determinative constellations of these two lunar mansions. T'ai-wei has no Western name as such because all the Chinese constellations were different from those seen by the Greeks. See Gustaaf Schlegel, *Uranographie Chinoise* (Leiden, 1875), p. 534. I owe this information to Professor Joseph Needham of Gonville and Caius College, Cambridge.

16   Somewhat condensed version of the legend in the *Chou-shu i-chi* 周書異記 as quoted by Fa-lin 法琳 (*T*. 52, 478b6; *T*. 53, 378b18–19, 1028a27–b4). *HJAS*, 15 (1952), 188–189, n. 94, and Zürcher, I, 273, II, 421. 此時無他 can also mean. "It does not affect us now."

17   粤四十二年 preceding this sentence is omitted in translation.

18   For a discussion of the age at which Śākyamuni left home *(pravrajita)* see Lamotte, I, 208, n. 1.

the tree, attained enlightenment, and expounded the Law for the benefit of living beings. It was as if the *udumbara* 優曇花[19] had made one of its appearances. He preached first the *Avataṃsaka*,[20] then the Hīnayāna [doctrine], or the *Prajñā[pāramitā]*[21] and *Sandhinirmocana*,[22] or the *Saddharmapuṇḍarīka*[23] and *Nirvāṇa*.[24] He bestowed benevolence on all, taking advantage of opportune conditions[25] to spread the teaching and matching his teaching to the peculiarities of each listener.[26] It was like one gust of wind causing ten

[19] Ficus glomerata, symbolizes the appearance of a Buddha in the world; said to blossom only once in 3,000 years (*T.* 10, 442c4). Lamotte, I, 304–305, n. 2.

[20] Of three translations into Chinese, the first (418–420), based on the Sanskrit version in 36,000 gāthā discovered in Khotan by Fa-ling betweeen 392 and 408, is that by Buddhabhadra (359–429; *KSC*, 50, 334b–335c; *T.* 55, 506c) at Nanking in 60 chapters. (*KT.* 8, 1a–424c; *T.* 9, 395a–788b). The second (695–699), by Śikṣānanda (652–710), in 80 chapters at Lo-yang, is based on the Sanskrit version in 40,000 gāthā brought over by him from Khotan in 695 (*KT.* 8, 425a–943c; *T.* 10, 1a–444c). The third (798) is by Prājña, in 40 chapters (*T.* 10, 661a–851c). See *TP*, 48 (1960), 61–74. For recent Japanese studies see, for example, Araki Kengo 荒木見悟, *Jukyō to bukkyō* (Kyoto, 1963), pp. 9–90; Nakamura Hajime and Kawada Kumatarō 中村元、川田熊太郎, eds., *Kegon shisō* 華嚴思想 (Kyoto, 1960); Sakamoto Yukio 坂本幸男, *Kegon kyōgaku no kenkyū* 華嚴教學の研究 (Kyoto, 1956), pp. 301–508; and Takamine Ryōshū 高峰了洲, *Kegon shisōshi* (Kyoto, 1963),

[21] For a bibliography on *Prajñāpāramitā* see Edward Conze, *The Prajñāpāramitā Literature* (The Hague, 1960). For the definition of the term see Lamotte, II, 650 ff.; for the etymology of the word *pāramitā* see *ibid.*, 701, n. 1; 1058, n. 2; 1066.

[22] Literally, "unfolding of the real truth" or "explanation of deep mystery." Translated by Hsüan-tsang in 647 (*KT.* 10, 709a–743a; *T.* 16, 688b–711b). According to *BKD*, III, 102c–103a, only the *Hae simmilgyŏng so* 解深密經疏 in 10 chapters by Wŏnch'ŭk survives (*Zokuzōkyō*, IA, 34, 291a–394c, 395a–476c; 35, 1a–50d).

[23] Of the three Chinese translations, the first is by Dharmarakṣa (265–316) in 10 chapters (*KT.* 9, 801a–897a; *T.* 9, 63a–134b); the second by Kumārajīva (406) in 8 chapters (*KT.* 9, 725a–800b; *T.* 9, 1a–62c); the third (601) is by Dharmagupta (d. 619) in 7 chapters (*KT.* 9, 899a–976b; *T.* 9, 134b–196a). For more on this sūtra in China see *MCB*, 12 (1962), 183–214.

[24] The Mahāyāna version was translated first by Fa-hsien and Buddhabhadra in 417–418 in 3 chapters (*KT.* 19, 157a–181a; *T.* 1, 191b–207c). Dharmakṣema's Northern version (414–421) was introduced to the South sometime in 420 (*CSTCC*, 15, 111a16), and the altered Southern version was prepared by Hui-yen (364–443; *KSC*, 7, 367b–368b, esp. 368b20–23), Hui-kuan (d. 443; *KSC*, 7, 368b), and Hsieh Ling-yün (J. D. Frodsham, International Association of Historians of Asia, *Proceedings of the Second Biennial Congress* [1962], pp. 50–51). The Northern version is in *KT.* 9, 1a–260a, and *T.* 12, 365a–603c; the altered Southern version is in *T.* 12, 605a–852b. See Zürcher, II, 412, n. 125, and *JAS*, 13 (1958), 72, n. 27.

[25] 機 "opportune conditions" or "fundamental ability," that is, the spiritual ability or state of mind which is able to be stirred by the teachings of the Buddha (cf. 機感相應有形言現 in *T.* 35, 108b10). See Wing-tsit Chan, *A Source Book in Chinese Philosophy*, p. 784, and *MBD*, I, 491c–493a.

[26] For 方圓 see *Mencius*, IVA, 1 (Legge, II, 288) and IVA, 2 (Legge, II, 292); also *Hsün tzu (SPTK)*, 7, 8b. The passages are reminiscent of those in *T.* 14, 538a2, 4 (Étienne Lamotte, *L'Enseignment de Vimalakīrti* [Louvain, 1962], pp. 109–110): "The Buddha preaches with one voice, but all beings understand according to their capacities." Here the listing of the *Avataṃsaka* and

thousand holes to resound or like the lonely moon casting its reflection upon a thousand rivers.[27] For forty-nine years he enlightened and saved men of various capacities. Lieh Tzu's "sage in the Western Regions"[28] was he. Meanwhile Mañjuśrī[29] and Mahāmaudgalyāyana 目連,[30] in order to convert men, planted their footprints on Chinese soil.[31] When Buddha was seventy-nine, on the fifteenth day of the second month of the year *jen-shen* 壬申 (949 B.C.) of King Mu 穆王,[32] he entered nirvāṇa in the grove of śāla trees 瓊林.[33] Twelve white rainbows appeared and stayed night after night in the sky. The king asked the Grand Astrologer Hu To 扈多 for an explanation, and the latter answered, "The great sage of the West has just entered nirvāṇa."

other texts is modeled after the tenet-classification (*p'an-chiao* 判教) system of the T'ien-t'ai sect (*MCB*, 12 [1962], 229–271).

27   See *Fa-hua hsüan-i*, IIA, *T*. 33, 697c17–18, and *Ta-chih-tu lun*, 4, *T*. 25, 93a10 (Lamotte, I, 298). A collection of devotional poems praising the life of Śākyamuni by King Sejong also bears the title *Wŏrin ch'ŏn'gang chigok* 月印千江之曲 (Songs of the Moon's Reflection on a Thousand Rivers), for which see my *Korean Literature: Topics and Themes* (Tucson, 1965), p. 34 and bibliography on p. 35.

28   *Lieh tzu (SPPY)*, 4, 4b–5a (A. C. Graham, *The Book of Lieh-tzu* [London, 1960], p. 78). Graham, in "The Date and Composition of Liehtzyy," *AM*, 8 (1961), 139–198, considers it a third-century forgery. See Yang Po-chün 楊伯峻, *Lieh-tzu chi-shih* 列子集釋 (Shanghai, 1958), pp. 185–245. "A sage in the West" and other passages have been cited as evidencing their origin in Buddhist works; hence the work is dated after the introduction of Buddhism into China. Others, like Ku Chieh-kang, question this kind of reasoning, however. See also Hian-lin Dschi, "Lieh-tzu and Buddhist Sutras," *Studia Serica*, 9 (1950), 18–32.

29   For the cult and characteristics of Mañjuśrī in general and the cult in India, Khotan, Nepal, and China see Étienne Lamotte, "Mañjuśrī," *TP*, 48 (1960), 1–96. Also M. Th. de Mallmann, *Étude iconographique sur Mañjuśrī* (Paris, 1964).

30   For this hero in the story of the origin of *ullambana* see *T*. 16, no. 685, and *JAOS*, 71 (1951), 71–75.

31   For 迹子 read 迹于, as in A1b8. For 震檀, as referring to China, see Pelliot (3), (4), and (8), pp. 264–278, and *SR*, 12 (1927), 36–45, 179–191. The term was used in Korea to refer to Manchuria and Korea, especially the latter. Up to the beginning of the 15th century it was written as 震旦, but during the reign of King T'aejo of the Yi it was written as 一檀 to avoid his tabu name Tan 旦. An instance of the latter occurs in the *Sindo pi* 神道碑 (Inscription on the Avenue to the Grave, 1409) of T'aejo's Kŏnwŏn Tomb 健元陵, drafted by Kwŏn Kŭn 權近 (1353–1409), for which see *Yangch'on chip* 陽村集 (1937 ed.), 36, 5a–12a; *CKS*, II, 732–738; and *TYS*, 11, 10a–15a. Yi Pyŏng-do 李丙燾, in an essay on this term in the first issue of the *Chindan hakpo* 震檀學報, dismisses the forced etymology advanced by Fa-yün 法雲 and Hui-lin 慧林, the former in *Fan-i ming-i chi* 翻譯名義集 3, *T*, 54, 1098b, and the latter in *I-ch'ieh-ching yin-i* 一切經音義 22, *T*. 54, 447c. See also *T*. 10, 241c, and 54, 939b. For Yi's article see *CH*, 1 (1934), 167–174. *CPT*, I, 3 reads: 爲人示跡于震旦.

32   See n. 16 to the Introduction.

33   When the World-Honored One passed into nirvāṇa in the śālavana in Kuśinagara, the twin śāla trees between which the Buddha was lying turned as white as the white crane, and the leaves, fruit, bark and, trunks all burst and fell. Hence the trees are also called 鶴樹, as, for example, in extant stone

Thereupon Ānanda and other disciples gathered and edited the Buddha's sayings and recorded them on pattra leaves.[34] The Buddha's teachings were organized into *sūtra*, *vinaya*, *śāstra*, *śīla*, *samādhi*, and *prajñā*,[35] which thus opened the way for their dissemination.[36] But the eternal truth of the *Avataṁsaka sūtra*[37] was buried in the Dragon Palace 虹宮.[38] Heterodox teachings flourished and competed clamorously with one another.[39] Later, however, Aśvaghoṣa 馬鳴[40] rose; then, when Dignāga 陳那 (ca. A.D. 400–480)[41] and

---

monuments of Buddhist origin dating from the Silla and Koryŏ periods (e.g., *CKS*, I, 162, 471) and in *SGYS*, 3, 151 (cf. *MBD*, I, 419a–b). Here Kakhun is perhaps trying to say that the śāla trees, because of their associations, are as beautiful as the white jade. See *Ta-po nieh-p'an-ching hou-fen* 大般涅槃經後分 1, *T.* 12, 905a8–12. A1b9 and *CPT*, I, 3, line 10, read 雙林. See also Odette Viennot, *Le culte de l'arbre dans l'Inde ancienne* (Paris, 1954), pp. 130 ff., esp. pp. 235–238.

34 For the compilation of the Buddha's sayings see, for example, *T.* 12, 1058a–b and 50, 301a. For pattra leaves see Lamotte, II, 939–942, and *HBGR*, pp. 47b–48a.

35 In the original, 經律論戒定慧. The first three, *sūtrānta-*, *vinaya-*, and *abhidharma-piṭaka*, constitute *trīṇi piṭakāni*. For the latter three, known as 三學 (*trīṇi śikṣāṇi*), see *A-p'i-ta-mo chü-she-lun* 阿毘達磨俱舍論 24, *T*, 29, 127a2–4 (Louis de la Vallée Poussin, *L'Abhidharmakośa de Vasubandhu*, IV [Louvain, 1925], 225); *Ta-ch'eng i-chang* 大乘義章 10, *T.* 44, 657c; *CSTCC*, 11, 80a. The fifth item is rendered *citta* in Vasubandhu; it is *dhyāna* when it refers to one of the six *pāramitās*.

36 爰方啓行: *Shih ching*, 250, (Bernhard Karlgren, *The Book of Odes* [Stockholm, 1950], p. 207). Cf. Arthur Waley, *The Book of Songs* (London, 1954), no. 239, p. 244.

37 In the original, 雜華恒常之説. 雜華, as referring to Hua-yen, occurs in the *Kyunyŏ chŏn* 均如傳, 8, 63, *CKS*, I, 75, 82, 141, 182, 185, 225, etc., and *SGYS*, 4, 193.

38 虹宮: when Nāgārjuna entered the sea through the intercession of a Mahānāgā, there he received the scriptures, recited them for ninety days, and comprehended their ultimate meaning. Hence, the term refers to the dragon palace in which he recited the scriptures, including ths Hua-yen sūtra. See Max Walleser, "The Life of Nāgārjuna from Tibetan and Chinese Sources," *AM*, Hirth Anniversary Volume (1922), 421–455, esp. 446–447, and *TP*, 48 (1960), 42, 43 (n. 84), and 62, where Lamotte quotes *T.* 51, 153c18–22, and 54, 1065c14 ff.

39 Compare 邪宗蚖肆, 異部蛙鳴 in the original with passages in *T.* 51, 1532c19–20: 佛初去後, 賢聖隨應, 異道競興 (*TP*, 48 [1960], 42 and n. 80 on the same page). Here the specific reference is to the split of the Order into eighteen (or twenty) schools after Gautama's death, for which see *I-pu tsung-lun lun* 異部宗輪論 in *T.* 49, 15a–17b (tr. Masuda Jiryō, in *AM*, 2 [1925], 1–78), and André Bareau, *Les sectes bouddhiques du petit véhicule* (Saigon, 1955), esp. pp. 42–51, where the author offers a number of possible reasons for such schism.

40 A learned Brahmin converted to Buddhism. For a bibliography on him see Yamada Ryūjō 山田龍城, *Bongo butten no shobunken* 梵語佛典の諸文献 (Tokyo, 1959), pp. 67–77, to which add Timothy Richard, *Ashvagosha, The Awakening of Faith* (London, reprinted 1961), a translation of the *Mahāyanā-śraddhotpāda śāstra* (cf. Walter Liebenthal, "New Light on the *Mahāyāna-śraddhopāda śāstra*," *TP*, 46 [1958], 155–216). For his biography by Kumārajīva see *T.* 50, no. 2046, 183a–184a; for an earlier study on him by Tokiwa Daijō 常盤大定 see his *Memyō bosatsu ron* 馬鳴菩薩論 (Tokyo, 1905).

41 A native of Andhra in South India and the author of the *Nyāyamukha*, translated in 711 by I-ching (*T.* 32, 6a–11a; *BKD*, I, 188c–d), the *Pramāṇasamuccaya*, etc.; *MBD*, IV, 3634c–3636a.

Dharmapāla 護法 (530–631)[42] preached in harmony,[43] the false [teachings] were discarded, the true [law] revealed itself, and the doctrine was extended and clarified. Buddhism was thus well established[44] in the Western Regions, and awaited [only] a proper occasion to spread eastward.

One hundred and sixteen years after the Buddha's demise, King Aśoka (268–232 B.C.)[45] of East India collected the Buddha's relics and mobilized spirit soldiers to erect 84,000 stūpas,[46] which extended all over [the continent of] Jambudvīpa.[47] This time was equivalent to the twenty-sixth year, *ting-wei* 丁未, of King Ching of Chou (494 B.C.).[48] The stūpas flourished during the Chou, lasting through [the reigns of] twenty-two kings,[49] but finally disappeared when the First Emperor of Ch'in (260–221–210 B.C.) burned the books in his thirty-fourth year (213 B.C.).[50] The stūpas of King Aśoka were thus destroyed. At that time, eighteen worthies, including śramaṇa Li-fang 利方,[51] carrying scriptures, came to convert [the people of] Hsien-

---

42 For Dharmapāla, one of the ten great authorities on Vijnaptimātra, see *MBD*, II, 1291c–1292b.

43 For 唱之和之 see *Hsün tzu*, 14, 4b (Homer H. Dubs, *The Works of Hsüntze* [London, 1928], p. 253).

44 悉備: *Chou i*, 8, 8b (Wilhelm, I, 377).

45 Grandson of Chandragupta Maurya (*ca.* 321–297 B.C.) and son of Bindusāra. For the following passages see and compare Tsukamoto, pp. 132 ff. (Hurvitz, pp. 42–43).

46 For Aśoka's erection of stūpas see *A-yu-wang chuan* 阿育王傳 1, *T.* 50, 102a14 (Jean Przyluski, *La Légende de l' Empereur Açoka* [Paris, 1923], p. 242) and *A-yu-wang ching*, 1, *T.* 50, 153a. See also Lamotte, *Histoire du Bouddhisme indien* (Louvain, 1958), pp. 259–283, esp. 263–264, and *TP*, 48 (1960), 58, n. 134. A feverish search for these alleged stūpas took place in China at one time owing to the belief that China, being a part of Jambudvīpa, must have been ruled over by Aśoka. Koreans, too, believed in this legend, as we can see from the *SGYS* and from Buddhist-inspired inscriptions on stone monuments dating from early periods. Chapter 24 of the *Sŏkpo sangjŏl* 釋譜詳節, for example, contends that among 84,000 stūpas, two are located in Korea, one on Mount Ch'ŏn'gwan 天冠山 in South Chŏlla and another on the Diamond Mountains. A volume printed in copper type containing chapters 23 and 24 of the *Sŏkpo sangjŏl* was made known to the academic world for the first time in 1966, for which see *Tongak ŏmun nonjip* 東岳語文論集, 5 (March 1967), 174–179.

47 One of the four continents situated south of Mount Sumeru, comprising the world known to the early Indians (*MBD*, I, 317a–b, and *HJAS*, 9, 258–259, n. 41).

48 The chronology here is hopelessly confused.

49 This passage is unintelligible.

50 For the burning of the books see *Shih chi*, 6, 0025c (*MH*, II, 171–174). According to Tung Tso-pin, *Chronological Tables of Chinese History*, it is the *wu-tzu* 戊子 year. Kakhun accepts the version in the *Shih chi*, 6, 0023a, that the First Emperor succeeded his father in 247 B.C. (*MH*, II, 98).

51 Or Shih Li-fang. This episode appears for the first time in *LTSPC* (597), *T.* 49, 23c. Professor Hurvitz writes that the original, 金剛丈人, for "a bearer of a vajra-staff" (two lines below), should read 金剛杖人.

yang 咸陽. But the First Emperor of Ch'in would not allow them to preach and imprisoned them. [1015c] At night, a bearer of the vajra-staff broke into the prison, released them, and went away, because the time for propagation was not yet ripe.

In the twelfth year of the era *yung-p'ing* (A.D. 69)[52] of the Later Han, [Kāśyapa] Mātaṅga 摩騰[53] and Dharmaratna 竺法蘭[54] arrived at the Han court. Compassionate clouds spread over the nine provinces[55] and the rain of compassionate Law fell on the four seas. According to the biography of Ho Ch'ü-ping 霍去病,[56] however, Ho obtained a "golden man" 金人[57] (120 B.C.), which King Hsiu-ch'u 休屠王 used in worshiping Heaven. Thus it appears that the worship of idols had long prevailed in the desert. [We also know that] during the reign of Emperor Ai (26-7-1 B.C.) of the Former Han (202 B.C.-A.D. 9) Ch'in Ching 秦景[58] was sent to the country of the Yüeh-chih[59] (2 B.C.) and that upon his return he transmitted the teaching of Buddha.[60] We conclude, therefore, that Buddhism had already been practiced

---

[52] This must be the eleventh year (A.D. 68); if not, it will introduce a fifth version for their arrival at the Han court. See Maspero (1), 125 and Zürcher, I, 22, 29–30; II, 325, n. 20. *CPT*, I, 4, line 4, reads "thirteenth year."

[53] Of Central Indian origin, he arrived in Lo-yang, worked at the White Horse monastery there, and died in A.D. 73. *KSC*, 1, 322a–323a (Maspero [1], 115–116).

[54] For the name Dharmaratna see Pelliot (5), 387–388, n. 1; for his biography see *KSC*, 1, 323a–324b (Maspero [1], 116–117).

[55] That is, China. For this see Arthur E. Link, *Oriens Extremus*, 8 (1961), 148, n. 59, and *MT*, I, 369d.

[56] Died 117 B.C. *Shih chi*, 111, 0248b ff. (Burton Watson, *Records of the Grand Historian of China* [2 vols; New York, 1961], II, 200–216, esp. 200–210); *Ch'ien Han shu*, 55, 0493d–0494d (Homer H. Dubs, *The History of the Former Han Dynasty*, II [Baltimore, 1944], 60 ff., 71); Zürcher, I, 21; II, 324–325; *BD*, 645.

[57] For the golden man see a bibliography in Ch'en, *Buddhism in China*, pp. 507–508. According to Dubs, II, 62, King Hsiu-ch'u died in the third year of the era *yüan-shou* of King Wu (121 B.C.).

[58] James R. Ware, "Wei Shou on Buddhism," *TP*, 30 (1933), 110–111, n. 7; Zürcher, I, 24–25; II, 326; *BEFEO*, 4 (1906), 375, n. 1; Chavannes (3), 547, n. 4, and 547–549; Tsukamoto, p. 86 (Hurvitz, p. 28); Pelliot (6), 390–392, n. 298.

[59] Of Indo-European speech (Tokharian). "It is certain . . . that they were the Tokhari of Strabo and Ptolemy," says Joseph Needham, *Science and Civilization in China*, I (Cambridge, 1954), 173, n. a. For their history see *Shih chi*, 110, 1014d (Watson, *Records of the Grand Historian of China*, II, 160 ff., 364 passim); *Ch'ien Han shu*, 86A, 0607b; *Hou Han shu*, 118, 0905a (Chavannes [4], 187–192); *MH*, I, 1 ff. For Buddhist practices among the Yüeh-chih see Hatani Ryōtai 羽溪了諦, *Saiiki no bukkyō* 西域の佛教 (Kyoto, 1914), pp. 81–194.

[60] For 浮屠 see *HBGR*, pp. 190a-197b; Tsukamoto, pp. 92–93; and n. 2 above.

in the Former Han. Only sixty-three years later did Emperor Hsiao-ming (A.D. 28–58–75) dream of "a golden man."[61]

As for our country Haedong 海東,[62] Sundo 順道 arrived in P'yŏngyang-sŏng 平壤城 during the reign of King Haemiryu 解味留王[63] (371–384) of Koguryŏ 高句麗. Following him, *Mālānanda 摩羅難陀[64] came to Paekche 百濟 from [Eastern] Chin (317–420) during the reign of King Ch'imnyu 枕流王[65] (384–385). Later, after the enthronement of the twenty-third king of Silla 新羅, Pŏphŭng 法興王[66] (514–540), on the eleventh day of the third month of the first year of the era *ta-t'ung* 大通 (April 27, 527) of Liang, Ado[67] arrived in Ilsŏn County 一善郡[68] and was secretly hidden by a believer, Morye 毛禮. The ambassador from Wu (222–280) brought incense as a gift,[69] and Ado, because he showed people the rites of burning incense, was invited to court. But the teaching of Buddhism was not yet expounded. The Grand Secretary Yŏmch'ok 厭髑 (503–527)[70] dispelled his countrymen's doubts by a brave martyrdom. Ah, were it not for him, what religion would

---

61   Maspero (1), 115–117, 120; Pelliot (6) says, on p. 263, "Le rêve de Ming-ti et l'ambassade qui l'aurait suivi sont légendaires, c'est entendu." See also Maspero (4), I, 195–211, and II, 185–199. *Konjaku monogatari* 今昔物語, chaps. 6 and 7 of which are devoted to Buddhist tales and traditions of China, contains a story, "How under Emperor Ming of the Later Han Buddhism Crossed to China." *Konjaku monogatari shū* (*Nihon koten bungaku taikei*, 23; Tokyo, 1960), 6, 54–56 (S. W. Jones, tr., *Ages Ago: Thirty-Seven Tales from the Konjaku Monogatari Collection* [Cambridge, 1959], pp. 35–38).

62   Kwŏn Mun-hae 權文海 (1534–1591), in his *Taedong unbu kunok* 大東韻府群玉, 1, 1a, quotes a gloss from the *Yongbi ŏch'ŏn ka* 龍飛御天歌, 1, 1a, where the term *Haedong* is explained: "Korea is called Haedong because it lies east of Po-hai (Parhae 渤海)."

63   Or Sosurim 小獸林 or Sohaejuryu 小解朱留, son of King Kogugwŏn 故國原王 (331–371), seventeenth king of Koguryŏ. He was succeeded by his brother Iyŏn 伊連 (King Kogugyang 故國壤王, 384–391). *SGSG*, 18, 3. For Sundo's biography see below.

64   *SGYS*, 3, 122, interprets his name to mean 童學. Iryŏn perhaps guessed that the original Sanskrit first syllable, ku, in *Kumāra* ("boy") was dropped; as for the second part of the compound, *nanda*, a common Indian name meaning "joy" or "happy," *nandi (n)* can be the second part of a name with the meaning of "son." See Ogihara Unrai, *Bonwa daijiten* 梵和大辭典 (Tokyo, 1940–1943, 1963–1966), pp. 357, 656. I owe this information to Professor Johannes Rahder of Yale University.

65   The eldest son of King Kŭn'gusu 近仇首王 (375–384). He was succeeded by his brother King Chinsa 辰斯王 (385–392). *SGSG*, 24, 6–7. For 千 read 于, as in A2b8.

66   See his biography below.

67   See his biography below.

68   Modern Sŏnsan 善山 in North Kyŏngsang (*TYS*, 29, 1b). For Morye see n. 214 below.

69   This chronology is impossible, unless Wu is metonymy for China. See n. 29 to the Introduction.

70   For his biography see the section on Pŏpkong. The passage 赤心面內 can also be read: "Facing the inner truth with sincerity."

I follow now? Since men like Wŏn'gwang 圓光 (d. 640)[71] and Chajang 慈藏 (fl. 636–645)[72] journeyed to the West and transmitted the Law, both high and low have believed in Buddhism, and people both within and without the court have followed and practiced it. As time went on, more and more responded and joined the faith. Buddhism thus became popular in the Three Han 三韓.[73]

Our August Progenitor[74] (877–918–943) dropped old customs and initiated reform;[75] he respected Buddhism especially, and most of his institutions were set up in accordance with that religion.[76] His heirs succeeded to the government and preserved its culture,[77] losing nothing. The National Preceptor Taegak 大覺國師 (1055–1101),[78] the fourth-generation descend-

---

71 See his biography below. He left Silla in 589 and returned in 600.

72 See n. 47 to the Introduction.

73 Mahan, Chinhan, Pyŏnhan. For more on these see n. 199 below.

74 The founder of the Koryŏ dynasty, Wang Kŏn 王建. *KRS*, 1, 1a–2, 19b; *KRSCY*, 1, 1a–46b.

75 For 革舊鼎 read 革舊鼎新, as in *CPT*, I, 4, line 12.

76 His Buddhist policy is best manifested in his "Ten Injunctions" (943), especially Articles 1, 2, 5, and 6 (*KRS*, 2, 14b–17a).

77 守文繼體之君 is 繼體守文之君 in the *Po-hu t'ung* 白虎通 (*SPTK*), 1, 12a (Tjan Tjoe Som, *Po Hu T'ung: The Comprehensive Discussions in the White Tiger Hall*, I [Leiden, 1949], 235).

78 His name was Hu 煦, his polite name, Ŭich'ŏn 義天. Born October 21, 1055, he was the fourth son of King Munjong 文宗 (1019–1047–1082–1983), the elventh king of Koryŏ. He became a bonze in the fifth month of 1065 and in the tenth month received the *Upasampadā*. In 1067 he was named the Chief of Clerics, with the pen name of Use 祐世, and in 1077 he began to lecture on Prājña's translation of the *Avataṁsaka* (40 chaps.). He left the Koryŏ capital on May 4, 1085, with his disciple Sugye 壽介 and others and went to Sung. He was soon joined by other disciples, such as Nakchin 樂眞 (*CKS*, I, 314–318; *KRS*, 13, 32b), Torin 道隣 (or Toryŏn 道憐), and Hyesŏn 彗宣. In Sung he studied the *Avataṁsaka* under Ching-yüan 淨源 (1011–1088; *T*. 49, 294a5–18, 672a–c, 877a), T'ien-t'ai under Tsung-chien 從諫 (d. January 19, 1110; *T*. 49, 218c10–219a2, 881c), Vināya and Pure Land under Yüan-chao 元照 (1048–1116; *T*. 49, 297b–c, 681a4–17, 877a–b), and Dhyāna under Liao-yüan 了元 (d. February 7, 1098; *T*. 49, 676c–677b). He returned after fourteen months in Sung China. He died October 28, 1101, and was buried on Mount Ogwan, east of the Yŏngt'ong monastery, on November 26, 1101. For his biography see *KRS*, 90, 1b–15a (*KRS*, 8, 27b; 11, 31a; 88, 9b); *CKS*, I, 293–295 (in the Hŭngwang monastery; erected in 1101), 305–316 (in the Yŏngt'ong monastery; erected in 1125), and 329–334 (in the Sŏnbong monastery 僊鳳寺 in North Kyŏngsang; erected in 1132); *T*.49, 223b–224a, 877 a–b. His works include a catalogue of scriptures and treatises, *Sinp'yŏn chejong kyojang ch'ongnok* 新編諸宗教藏總錄 (*T*. 55, 1165b–1178c); *Wŏnjong mullyu* 圓宗文類, of which only chapters 1, 14, 21, and 22 survive (the Kanazawa Bunko edition of chap. 21 was published in *Butsudai gakuhō* 佛大學報, 30 [1955], 105–121), an anthology which was imported into Japan before 1094 and was widely studied by monks of the Kegon School; and *Sŏgwŏn sarim* 釋苑詞林, of which only a volume containing chaps. 191–195 of the original 250 chapters survives. Finally, *Taegak kuksa munjip* 大覺國師文集 (1931), a posthumous compilation of his writings, exists in two volumes, and their wood blocks are preserved in the Haein monastery. For his works see Ōya Toku-

ant of T'aejo,[79] seeking the Law, sailed eastward in the fourth month of the third year,[80] *ŭlch'uk* 乙丑, of King Sŏn[jong] 宣宗 (1049–1084–1094).[81] He guided a hundred schools, each to its proper place, within the Five Doctrines,[82] so that once again they reverted to orthodoxy.

[Buddhism] therefore had its source in Chou, formed streams in Han, became broad and deep in Chin and Wei (220–265), overflowed in Sui (589–618) and T'ang (618–906), undulated in Sung (960–1279), and gushed in swift commotion in Korea.[83] Since Buddha's nirvāṇa to the present year, *ŭrhae* 乙亥 (1215), 2,164 years have passed. It has been 1,151 years since Buddhism was introduced into the Later Han, 1,014 years after Buddha's demise. And since Sundo came to Koguryŏ[84] it has been 844 years. The Law cannot promulgate itself; it must be propagated by men.[85] I therefore wrote

---

jō 大屋德城, *Kōrai zokuzō chūzōkō* 高麗續藏雕造攷 (3 vols; Kyoto, 1937); Cho Myŏng-gi, *Koryŏ Taegak kuksa wa Ch'ŏnt'ae sasang* (1964); Kim Sang-gi 金庠基, "Taegak kuksa Ŭich'ŏn e taehayŏ," *Kuksasang ŭi chemunje*, 3 (1959), 79–102; Naitō Shunpo 內藤雋輔, in *Chōsen-shi kenkyū* (Kyoto, 1961), pp. 1–80; Takahashi Tōru, *CG*, 10 (1956), 113–147. Paul Demiéville, in his "Les versions chinoises du Milindapañha," *BEFEO*, 24 (1924), 199–206, esp. 201, mistranslates the term 微服 as "Ŭich'ŏn's disciple." It is an adverb meaning "in disguise" or "stealthily." For 國師 see Pelliot (2); and Hsü Ching 徐兢, *Hsüan-ho feng-shih Kao-li t'u-ching* 宣和奉使高麗圖經 (Keijō, 1932), 18, 95–96 (cf. *Sung shih*, 204, 4994b).

79 For 大祖 read 太祖.

80 Should be the second year (1085); the cyclical sign is correct.

81 In the original 宣王, for which see *KRS*, 10, 1a–31b, and *KRSCY*, 6, 1a–20a.

82 Should read 小大始終頓圓之五教. This is the famous Hua-yen classification of the Buddha's teachings according to the nature of his listeners: (1) teaching of the śrāvakas; (2) elementary doctrine of the Great Vehicle; (3) final doctrine of the Great Vehicle; (4) abrupt doctrine of the Great Vehicle; and (5) round doctrine of the Great Vehicle. See Fa-tsang's 法藏, *Hua-yen wu-chiao chang* 華嚴五教章 in *T.* 50, 285a6–8. Ch'oe Ch'i-wŏn 崔致遠, in his biography of Fa-tsang, refers to this as *Chiao-fen chi* 教分記 (*T.* 50, 282c16). See also *T.* 35, 115c5–6; 45, 481a7–8, 509a ff.; 48, 618c4–6, and P'yowŏn 表員, *Hwaŏmgyŏng munŭi yogyŏl mundap* 華嚴經文義要決文答 (*Zokuzōkyō*, IA, 12, 348a–b).

83 There is a parallel passage in a letter of Ching-yüan to the National Preceptor Taegak, in *Taegak kuksa munjip*, *woejip*, 2, 4b3–4: 源乎周,派于漢 … 汪洋於隋唐,瀞滿於炎宋. Compare Kakhun's periodization of Chinese Buddhism with, for example, that of A. F. Wright in *JAS*, 17 (1957), 19, and that of Kenneth K. S. Ch'en in *Buddhism in China*.

84 The name of Koguryŏ was variously written as Kuryŏ 句麗 (*SGYS*, 1, 51), Koryŏ, or Korye 高禮 (*Chewang un'gi* 帝王韻記, in *SGYS*, Appendix, 51). The noun is reconstructed to read *kol* or *kot*, and is compared to the Manchu *holo* in Lee Ki-moon, "A Comparative Study of Manchu and Korean," *Ural-Altaische Jahrbücher*, 30 (1958), 112, and Yang, p. 155. Throughout the translation I have rendered Kugoryŏ.

85 This statement is strongly reminiscent of the passages in Seng-yu's preface to *CSTCC*, 1, 1a (*JAOS*, 80 [1960], 37), where he says: "But the Way is aggrandized by man, and the Law awaits opportune conditions to be manifested."

this section on "propagators" for the sake of posterity. The biographies of eminent monks of Liang, T'ang, and Sung all have [sections on] translators; but since no translation has been made in our country I have omitted such a section.

Sundo

[1016a] Sŏk[86] Sundo's origin is unknown. He vigorously practiced virtue, towered above others in character,[87] and was compassionate and patient in helping living beings. He made a vow to propagate Buddhism and traveled extensively in China. He constantly moved his abode to meet opportunities and never tired of teaching others. During the sixth month of the summer in the second year (372), *imsin* 壬申, of the seventeenth king, Haemiryu (or Sosurim 小獸林, 371–384) of Koguryŏ, Fu Chien 苻堅 (338–357–385)[88] of Ch'in (351–394) dispatched an envoy and the monk Sundo with images of Buddha and scriptures. Thereupon the king and his court welcomed them in front of the palace gate[89] with appropriate ceremony[90] and, grateful for the opportunity to spread the faith, the king [showed] Sundo sincere respect and trust. Immediately afterwards the king sent an envoy with a tribute of local products to express his gratitude.[91] Another story holds that Sundo came from the Eastern Chin (317–420) and [that his visit] was the first time Buddhism was introduced [to Korea]. It is, therefore, unsolved whether he came from Ch'in or Chin.[92]

---

86 It was Tao-an 道安 who first thought that since Śākyamuni was the primary teacher of all monks, every monk should take the surname Shih (Śākya); Kakhun is of course following this practice. See *KSC*, 5, 353a1–2 (*TP*, 46 [1958], 28–29).

87 For 邁德 see *Shang shu* (*SPTK*), 2, 2b (Legge, III, 578); for 高標 see *Tu Shao-ling chi hsiang-chu* 杜少陵集詳註 (*WYWK*), 2, 59 (Erwin Von Zach, *Tu Fu's Gedichte* [Cambridge, 1952], I, 27, and William Hung, *Tu Fu* [Cambridge, 1952], p. 73).

88 His *tzu* was Yung-ku 永固 and his *ming*, Wen-yü 文玉. He was a son of Fu Hsiung, or a second son of Hsiung. See *Chin shu*, 113, 1372c–114, 1378c; *BD*, 579; Michael C. Rogers, "The Rise of the Former Ch'in State and Its Spread under Fu Chien through 370 A.D. (Based on *Chin shu* 113)" (unpublished Ph. D. thesis, University of California, Berkeley, 1953). Professor Rogers tells me that *Chin shu* is silent about this event.

89 I have rendered 省門 as palace gate, following *MT*, VIII, 186a.

90 會遇之禮: *Shih chi*, 47, 0161c (*MH*, V, 321, n. 1), and Séraphin Couvreur, *Li Ki ou Mémoires sur les Bienséances et les Cérémonies* (Hokienfou, 1913), p. 92: "les rites des entrevues."

91 *Chin shu*, 113, is silent about this event. *Chin shu*, 7, however, records such tribute missions in 336 (1094a), 343 (1094c), and 413 (1100b). *T'ung tien* 通典 (*Kuo-hsüeh chi-pen ts'ung-shu* ed.; Taipei, 1959), 185, 988b, records that in 382 a Silla king sent an envoy to offer beautiful girls. *T'ai-p'ing yü-lan* 太平御覽 (1807 ed.), 781, 6a, repeats the same. On the other hand, *SGSG*, 18, 3, records that in 377 King Sosurim sent an envoy to Fu Chien.

92 See Suematsu Yasukazu, *Shiragi-shi no shomondai* (Tokyo, 1964), pp. 207–225, and n. 22 to the Introduction.

When the master came to the foreign country, he transmitted the Compassionate Lamp of the Western Regions and hung up the Wisdom-Sun in Tong'i 東曀.[93] He demonstrated [the principle of] cause and effect and enticed [the people by predicating] felicity and woe as rewards for their deeds. As if imbued with fragrance and nourished by dew, people gradually became accustomed to his teaching. Unfortunately, however, the society was too simple and the people too unsophisticated to cultivate the faith. Despite the fact that his accumulated wisdom was profound and his explication broad, he did not manage to spread the religion very far. It was then more than 200 years since Kāśyapa Mātaṅga had come to the Later Han (A.D. 64).

Four years later, the divine monk Ado arrived from Wei,[94] and it was then that the Sŏngmun monastery 省門寺[95] was erected for Sundo. The record states that the monastery was built where the palace gate used to be.[96] It is the present Hŭngguk monastery 興國寺. Later, it was wrongly recorded as Ch'omun 肖門. In addition, in order to install Ado, the people built the Ibullan monastery 伊弗蘭寺,[97] which, according to the ancient record,[98] was the present Hŭngbok monastery 興福寺. This was the beginning of Buddhism in Korea.

What a waste of the man and his excellences![99] For there should be records on bamboo and silk glorifying his admirable accomplishment. Yet only a

---

93 Originally the capital of Lin-t'un 臨屯 prefecture, but later attached to Lo-lang 樂浪: here and elsewhere used as a metonym for Korea. See *Ch'ien Han shu*, 28B, 0426c.

94 See n. 29 to the Introduction.

95 According to *MBD*, III, 2796a–b, this is located in Ansisŏng 安市城 (*SGYS*, 3, 121). *SGSG*, 18, 3, says, "erected in the second month [March 19-April 16] of 375."

96 Here perhaps Kakhun had in mind the origin of a monastery in China in the Hung-lou Office 鴻臚寺. Fukui Kōjun suggests that the Buddhist place of worship was originally called 祠 (cf. *Shih chi*, 6, 0025b; *San-kuo chi, Wu chih*, 4, 1014b17; *Hou Han shu*, 72, 0791b and 0765b). But when the Ch'in established *chih* 畤 (**d'iəg*) as a place where the Five Emperors and Shang-ti were worshiped, the Buddhists decided to distinguish their place of worship from those of other deities of native origin and adopted the logograph 寺 (**dziəg*). *Tōyō shisōshi kenkyū* (Tokyo, 1960), pp. 186–197. For Po-ma ssu as the place where Mataṅga stayed see Maspero (1), 107, n. 3, 116, 117; *Shih-lao chih* (Hurvitz, pp. 29–30, n. 8); *Mou tzu, T.* 52, 5a4–5 (Pelliot [6], 311, 394, n. 304). *SGSG*, 18, 3, writes 肖門, but *SGYS*, 3, 121, refutes it.

97 Location unknown.

98 For 古記, rendered as "ancient" or "old" record, see *Changwoe chamnok*, I, 69, and *SGYS*, Introduction, pp. 15, 22–23.

99 之人也之德也 is a phrase used in *Chuang tzu*, 1, 13b (Burton Watson, *Chuang Tzu: Basic Writings* [New York, 1964], p. 27), to describe the Taoist saint who scorns the elements of Nature.

[small] number of his writings remain; one wonders why this is so. Only those who are wise are capable of carrying out a mission from the West without falling short of an imperial order.[100] As for going to a foreign country and there initiating a great religion which has hitherto not existed, one could not expect to succeed unless one was endowed with great wisdom and wise counsel[101] and the ability to employ supernatural religious powers at will. Thus we know Sundo must have been an unusual person, a peer of Dharmaratna and Seng-hui.[102]

The eulogy says:[103] In the past the Three Han stood like a tripod, each establishing its realm and proclaiming its king. There were as yet no omens, whether in sound or sight, of the glorious Buddha. When the stimulus and its response met, then a man of superior virtue arrived and, attracted by the potentialities [of our countrymen], tested them.[104] The *Book of Changes* says: "If the changes are stimulated, they penetrate all situations under Heaven."[105] Sundo understood this truth.

At first, my ambition was to write down events, having come to understand this as the way to make the country and Buddhism prosper. But I had not the opportunity to do so. Now that I have received the royal order,[106] unworthy as I am, I have begun the *Lives* with a biography of Sundo.

---

100 使於西方不辱君命: *Analects*, XIII, 20 (Arthur Waley, *The Analects of Confucius* [London, 1949], p. 176).

101 大謀猷: *Shang shu*, 11, 5a (Legge, III, 540): "plans and counsels."

102 For Seng-hui's biography see *KSC*, 1, 325a–326b, and Chavannes (5), See also Zürcher, I, 51–55 and 337, n. 150.

103 In the original this eulogy follows the biography of Mangmyŏng, a Koguryŏ monk; in the translation I have changed the order appropriately.

104 For 機叩 see n. 25 above.

105 感而遂通, 天下之故: *Chou i*, 7, 9a (Wilhelm, I, 339).

106 景命: *Shih ching*, 247, 7 (Karlgren, p. 204): "great appointment."

Mangmyŏng

Sŏk Mangmyŏng 釋亡名 was a native of Koguryŏ. He concentrated in the attainment of the Way and abided by benevolence. He cherished the truth and based his conduct on moral power. He remained unsoured even when his merits were unrecognized by others.[107] He cultivated virtue to such an extent that his reputation was invariably high in his own country; morever, his fame overflowed and spread even beyond his native land.[108] The Master of the Law[109] Chih Tun 支遁[110] (314–366) of Chin sent him a letter saying:[111] "The honorable monk Chu Fa-shen 竺法深 (286–374) was a disciple of Master Liu Yüan-chen 劉元眞[112] of Chung-chou 中州. With an upright and lofty nature, he was a controlling force over both the clergy and the laity. Formerly, while in the capital, he maintained the religious standards[113] and was respected both by people inside and outside the circle[114] as a master in propagating the way." Since [Chih] Tun [1016b] was a famous person in China, his associates must all have been of great talent and importance. In the case of a foreigner, had he not been superior even to them, how could he have been treated thus?

Moreover, after the introduction of Buddhism into Korea from Chin, there must have been heroic personages during the times of Sung and Ch'i, but regrettably no record of them exists. When Chu Ling-ch'i 朱靈期[115] of

---

107 人不知而不慍: *Analects*, I, 1 (Waley, p. 83).

108 In the original 考鐘于內, 在邦必聞, 霈然有餘, 厥聞旁馳. For the second phrase see *Analects*, XII, 20 (Waley, p. 168); for the third phrase see *Mencius*, IVA, 6 (Legge, II, 296).

109 法師: *Dharmabhāṇaka* or *dharmakathika*. See *MBD*, X, 954b–c; *BHSD*, p. 280a.

110 See n. 19 to the Introduction.

111 For his letter to a Koguryŏ monk (*KSC*, 4, 348a13–15) see Liu I-ch'ing, *Shih-shuo hsin-yü* 世說新語 (*SPPY*), 1A, 8b; Zürcher, II, 360–361, n. 213.

112 Teacher of Chu Fa-shen (286–374). See Zürcher, I, 77–75; *KSC*, 4, 347c-348b.

113 *KSC*, 4, 348a, has 體德 for ——性 and 法網 for ——綱.

114 Or by the laity and the religious alike.

115 Kakhun's gloss reads "or Chu Ling-hsü" 朱靈虛. According to *KSC*, 10, 391b–c, Chu Ling-ch'i was a native of Wu district, and on his way home from a diplomatic mission to Koguryŏ he encountered a storm. After nine days at sea he finally landed on an island with a high mountain. He entered the mountains, following a path he had discovered, and came upon a monastery. There he and his men worshiped some ten monks made of stone, but, upon hearing their chanting, Chu

[Liu] Sung (420–479) returned as an envoy from Koguryŏ, he was ship-wrecked and stranded on an island and there he obtained the begging bowl of Pei-tu 杯度.[116]

It is also said that during the Ch'i (479–502), people in Korea were still unaware of the birth of Buddha. Someone asked the eminent monk Fa-shang 法上 (495–580)[117] about it, and he replied by relating an auspicious omen that had occurred during the reign of King Chao of Chou. Therefore, lofty persons and famous gentlemen in China must have laughed at our ignorance. In truth, however, a number of people inquired about the essentials of Buddhism. What is really regrettable is that no good historian kept a detailed record.

---

realized that they were arhats and confessed his sins. After feasting on the vegetables the arhats had prepared for them, Chu and his men wanted to return home. An arhat asked Chu whether he knew Pei-tu 杯度. When Chu said he did, the arhat pointed to the northern wall, upon which hung a sack with a monk's staff and a bowl. With these objects Chu was able to find his way, entering the Huai safely. It is also interesting to note that Ling-ch'i was a popular name under the Northern Wei. See Yang Lien-sheng, "Lao-chün yin-sung chieh-ching chiao-shih," *Chung-yang yen-chiu-yüan li-shih yü-yen yen-chiu-so chi-k'an* 中央研究院歷史語言研究所集刊, 28 (1956), 17 ff., esp. 26, 37–38.

116 *KSC*, 10, 390b–392b (*MBD*, III, 2614c; *A Dictionary of Chinese Mythology* [Shanghai, 1932], pp. 369–371). *Chung-kuo jen-ming ta-tz'u-tien*, p. 579a, says: "Often crossed the water in a wooden cup, hence his name. He ignored trivialities and possessed extraordinary power of magic."

117 Chief of Clerics under the Northern Wei and Northern Ch'i; Preceptor of Northern Ch'i's Wen-hsüan. Versed in the *Nirvāṇa* and *Laṅkāvatāra* sūtras. *HKSC*, 8, 485a–486a; *LTSPC*, 12, 104c–105a.

Ŭiyŏn

Sŏk Ŭiyŏn 釋義淵 was a native of Koguryŏ. Nothing about his origin and lineage is known. After he shaved his head and became a monk,[118] he adhered well to the monastic rules. He possessed profound understanding and broad learning and comprehended the subtlety of Confucianism and *hsüan-hsüeh* (mysterious, or dark, learning).[119] He was in his time a leader of both monks and laymen. He loved to propagate the Law, his desire being the spread of Buddhism. Yet the supreme Law was difficult indeed to reveal in its true glory, and he was unable to discern the cause.

It was known that[120] monk Fa-shang of the Ting-kuo monastery 定國寺 in the Former Ch'i (550–577) was a leader of men and of all sentient beings, with his discipline firm as a mountain and his wisdom pure as the sea. He had been the Chief of Clerics for the entire realm of Ch'i, in charge of no fewer than two million monks and nuns for nearly forty years. During the reign of Emperor Wen-hsüan 文宣 (529–550–559)[121] he expounded the Buddhist canon splendidly, and both the clergy and laity glorified the truth; his great deeds[122] shone brightly, and his wonderful influence was far-reaching.[123]

At that time the Prime Minister of Koguryŏ, Wang Ko-dŏk 王高德,[124] had deep faith in the orthodox doctrine and respected Mahāyāna Buddhism. He desired to spread the influence of Buddhism over this corner of the sea. But because he was ignorant of the origin and development of the religion and of the reign period in which it had been introduced from the West, he listed

---

118 *CPT*, I, 16, line 9, substitutes 肄 for 隸, meaning 習. For 剃染 see *MBD*, IV, 3764c.

119 *CPT*, I, 16, reads 賢 instead of 玄. For *hsüan-hsüeh* see Fung Yu-lan, *A History of Chinese Philosophy*, II (Princeton, 1953), 168 ff.; Chan, *A Source Book in Chinese Philosophy*, pp. 314–335; Zürcher, II, 348, n. 12.

120 The following passages, beginning here and continuing to "I have recorded only the most important points," are almost verbatim quotations from *LTSPC*, 12, 104c9–105a8.

121 *Pei shih*, 7, 2763d–2766a; *Pei Ch'i shih*, 4, 2206a–2209a.

122 景行: *Shih ching*, 218 (Karlgren, p. 172).

123 逸響: *Wen hsüan* 文選 (*WYWK*), 35, 81 (Erwin von Zach, *Die Chinesische Anthologie* [Cambridge, 1958], II, 630).

124 A5b10 reads 丞相 for 聖相. I cannot identify him.

the following questions and sent [Ŭi] yŏn to Yeh[125] by sea in order to enlighten him. The general contents of the inquiry went as follows:[126] "How many years has it been since Śākyamuni entered nirvāṇa? How many years had passed in India before Buddhism was introduced into China? Who was the emperor when it was first introduced? What was his reign title? Also, in your opinion, which state first adopted Buddhism, Ch'i or Ch'en? [1016c] Please indicate the number of years and emperors since the practice of Buddhism began. Who wrote the treatises on the *Daśabhūmi, Prajñāpāramitā, Bodhisattvabhūmi,* and *Vajracchedika-prajñāpāramitā?* Was there any biography relating who originated or inspired the composition of these scriptures? I have recorded these questions and await your investigation to cast off my doubts."

[Fa-]shang answered thus: "The Buddha was born in the twenty-fourth years, *chia-yin* (1027 B.C.), of King Chao of Chou whose clan name was Chi 姬.[127] He left home at nineteen and became enlightened at thirty.[128] In the twenty-fourth year, *kuei-wei* (977 B.C.), of King Mu of Chou, the king heard of one from the West who had been transformed into a human being [in order to enlighten living beings], and who had then gone to the West and never returned.[129] Judging from this, Śākyamuni was in this world for forty-nine years. Since his nirvāṇa to the present, the seventh year, *ping-shen* (A.D. 576), of the era *wu-p'ing* 武平 of Ch'i, it has been 1,465 years. The scriptures and doctrines of Buddhism were first brought to China during the era *yung-p'ing* (58–75) of Emperor Ming of the Later Han and handed down through Wei and Chin. But it was not until the arrival of K'ang Seng-hui 康僧會 at Wu during the era *ch'ih-wu* 赤烏 (238–250) of Sun Ch'üan 孫權

---

125   Forty *li* southwest of Lin-chang hsien in North Honan; capital of Former Yen (348–370), Later Chao (319–352), Eastern Wei (534–550), and Northern Ch'i (550–577). For the city's history from the beginning to 577, when it fell to the army of the Northern Chou, see Miyakawa Hisayuki 宮川尚志, *Rikuchōshi kenkyū* 六朝史研究 (Tokyo, 1956), pp. 537–546.

126   The following quotation as far as "Who wrote the treatises on the *Daśabhūmi* . . ." is from *HKSC*, 8, 485b.

127   Chi was the clan name of the ruling house of Chou. See *Shih chi*, 4, 0013a (*MH*, I, 211, n. 3). Cf. *Lun heng* 論衡 (*SPPY*), 3, 21b (Alfred Forke, *Lun heng. Philosophical Essays of Wang Ch'ung* [2 vols.; London, 1907], I, 318).

128   For a discussion of the age at which the Buddha attained enlightenment see Lamotte, I, 179. As to whether he left home at nineteen or twenty-nine years of age, see references in n. 14 above.

129   I think this refers to the Buddha, not to King Mu's fabulous journey.

(182–222–252)[130] of Wu that the teaching of Buddhism was spread and propagated. Bhikṣu Asaṅga[131] received a copy of the *Bodhisattvabhūmi* from Maitreya, and during the era *lung-an* 隆安 (397–401) of Emperor An (383–397–418)[132] of Eastern Chin it was translated by T'an-mo-ch'an 曇摩讖 (Dharmakṣema, 385–433)[133] at Ku-tsang 姑藏[134] for the king of Ho-hsi 河西王, Chü-ch'ü Meng-hsün 沮渠蒙遜 (373–401–433).[135] The *Mo-ho-yen lun* 摩訶衍論[136] was written by Bodhisattva Nāgārjuna (ca. 100–200)[137] and translated, on the order of Yao Hsing 姚興 (394–416),[138] by Kumāra-

---

130 Proclaimed emperor in May 229; moved his capital from Wu-ch'ang (221–229) to Chien-yeh in 229. *San-kuo chih, Wu-chih*, 2, 1033c–1037c; *BD*, 1803.

131 The founder of the Idealistic school, author of the *Yogācārabhūmi* 瑜伽師地論, translated by Hsüan-tsang in 648 in 100 chapters (*KT*. 15, 530b–1408c; *T*. 30, 279a–882a), and of the *Bodhisattvabhūmi* 菩薩地持經 (8 or 10 chapters), translated by Dharmakṣema between 414 and 436 (*KT*. 14, 71a–160b; *T*. 30, 888a–959b).

132 *Chin shu*, 10, 1099a–1100c.

133 Eminent translator and propagator of Buddhism during the Northern Liang (401–439). A native of Kashmir (*Wei shu*, 114, 2195c) or of Central India (preface to *Mahāparinirvāṇa sūtra*, *T*. 12, 365b), he went to Ku-tsang via Tun-huang and was well received by Chü-ch'ü Meng-hsün. His translations include several disciplinary texts. *KSC*, 2, 335c–337c; *CSTCC*, 14, 102c; Tsukamoto, pp. 188–190, n. 2 (Hurvitz, pp. 58–59).

134 Modern Liang-chou in central Kansu.

135 Ruler of the Northern Liang. *Wei shu*, 99, 2122a–2123a; *Chih shu*, 129, 1404a–1405b; *Pei shih*, 93, 3030a–c; *Sung shu*, 98, 1657b–1658a; Alexander Soper, "Northern Liang and Northern Wei in Kansu," *Artibus Asiae*, 21 (1958), 131–164.

136 According to tradition, translated by Kumārajīva between 402 and 405 in 100 chaps. (*KT*. 374a–1379a; *T*. 25, 57a–756c). In addition to Lamotte's translation of chaps. 1–30, in *Le Traitéde la Grande Vertu de Sagesse de Nāgārjuna* (Louvain, 1944–1949), see Hikata Ryūshō, ed., *Suvikrāntavikrami pariprcchā Prajñāpāramitā-sūtra* (Fukuoka, 1958), pp. xii–xxvii, lii–lxxv; E. Conze, *The Prajñāpāramitā Literature*, p. 163. See also Miyamoto Shōson 宮本正尊, "Shōjo shuron no kenkyū: Tendai Kajō ni okeru Shina bukkyō no ichimondai," *Bukkyō kenkyū*, 2 (1938), 25.

137 *T*. 50, 184a–196c, and Walleser, "The Life of Nāgārjuna." For his ideas and works see Hayashiya, *Bukkyō oyobi bukkyōshi no kenkyū*, pp. 193–330, and Richard H. Robinson, "Some Logical Aspects of Nāgārjuna's System," *Philosophy East and West*, 6 (1957), 291–308, and *Early Mādhyamika in India and China* (Madison, 1967), pp. 21–70.

138 Unlike other non-Chinese rulers in the North, Yao Hsing was fond of learning, both Chinese (*Chin shu*, 117, 1382c) and Buddhist. Already during his stay in Ch'ang-an in his teens, he had shown a predilection for Buddhism. His zeal increased during his tenure as Heir Apparent of Yao Ch'ang. He was familiar with such scriptures as *Prajñāpāramitā* (*T*. 55. 53b5–7), *Vimalakīrtinirdeśa* (*T*. 55, 58b7–14), and *Saddharmapuṇḍarīka*, and keenly felt the deficiencies in available translations. He gave positive aid to the translation projects headed by Kumārajīva in order to produce more accurate versions of existing works and to introduce works hitherto unknown in China. Thus he eagerly encouraged the development of doctrinal studies in his kingdom of Later Ch'in. See Moroto Tatsuo 諸戸立雄, *Tōyōgaku*, 6 (Sendai, 1961), 35–48.

jīva (344–413)[139] upon his arrival in Ch'ang-an during the era *lung-an* of Chin. The treatises on the *Daśabhūmi* 十地論[140] and *Vajracchedikā-prajñāpāra-mitā* 金剛般若論[141] were compiled by the monk's brother Vasubandhu 波藪槃豆[142] and first translated by Bodhiruci 菩提留支[143] during the reign of Emperor Hsüan-wu 宣武 (483–500–515)[144] of the [Northern] Wei.''

In answering these queries, [Fa-] shang offered evidence and drew references from a wide range of sources. Here I have recorded only the most important points. [Ŭi] yŏn did not forget[145] the answers for a moment, had superior skill in leading people, and was versed in the mysterious and arcane. His ability in exegesis was inexhaustible, and his reason could master the secret of the joined circles.[146] Once dispelled, former doubts melted away like ice. Now this new, wonderful doctrine shines brilliantly like the dawn, obtaining the Wisdom-Sun in the West and pouring the fountain of Law into the East. His teaching, like a gold pendant or a string of gems, is imperish-

---

139 According to Tsukamoto, his dates are 350–*ca.* 409. He arrived in Ch'ang-an on February 8, 402, stayed there under Yao Hsing, and became the founder of the Mādhyamika school in China. *Chin shu*, 95, 1332d–1333b; *CSTCC*, 14, 100a–102a; *BD*, 1017. For the translation of his biography in *KSC*, 2, 330a–33a, see Johannes Nobel, ''Kumārajīva,'' *Sitzungsberichte der Preussischen Akademie der Wissenschaften*, 20 (1927), 206–233. See also Robinson, *Early Mādhyamika in India and China*, pp. 71–95.

140 In 12 chapters (*KT*. 15, 120a–237c; *T*. 26, 123a–203b).

141 There are three Chinese translations: (1) by Kumārajīva in one chapter (*KT*. 5, 979a–984b; *T*. 8, 748c–752c); (2) by Bodhiruci in 509 in one chapter (*KT*. 5, 985a–991b; *T*. 8, 752c–761c); and (3) by Paramārtha (499–569) between 558 and 569 (*KT*. 5, 993a–999c; *T*. 8, 762a–766c). See Conze, *The Prajñāpāramitā Literature*, for annotated bibliography and Ui Hakuju 宇井伯壽, *Daijō butten no kenkyū* 大乘佛典の研究 (Tokyo, 1963), pp. 3 ff.

142 The dates of Vasubandhu are something of a problem. According to Erich Frauwallner, *On the Date of the Buddhist Master of the Law Vasubandhu* (Rome, 1951), the elder's dates are 320–380 and the younger's, 400–480. Hattori Masaaki 服部正明, ''Jinna oyobi sono shūhen no nendai,'' *Tsukamoto hakushi shōju kinen bukkyō shigaku ronshū* (Kyoto, 1961), proposes 470–530; Hikata Ryūsyō, ''Seshin nendai saikō,'' *Miyamoto Shōson kyōju kanreki kinen rombunshū*(Tokyo, 1954), p. 321, proposes 440–520. For the study of his thought see Kudō Jōshō, 工藤成性 *Seshin kyōgaku no taikeiteki kenkyū* (Kyoto, 1955), and Yūki Reimon 結城令聞, *Seshin yuishiki no kenkyū* (Tokyo, 1955) and *Yuishikigaku tensekishi* (Tokyo, 1962). For the translation of his biography in *T*. 50, 188a–191a, see Takakusu Junjirō, ''The Life of Vasu-bandhu by Paramārtha (A.D. 499–569),'' *TP*, 5 (1904), 269–296.

143 菩提留(流)支 or 道晞. Lived in the largest monastery in Lo-yang, Ying-ning monastery, and between 508 and 535 translated 39 items comprising 129 chapters (*LTSPC*, 9, 85b–86b). For his biography see *HKSC*, 1, 428a–429c.

144 *Pei shih*, 4, 2754b–2755b; *Wei shu*, 8, 1921d–1924c.

145 服膺: *Chung yung*, 8 (Legge, I, 389).

146 連環: *Nan-hua chen-ching* 南華眞經 *(SPTK)* 10, 39b (Herbert A. Giles, *Chuang Tzu* [London, 1961], p. 322) and *Po-hu t'ung (SPTK)*, 7, 7a (Tjan, *Po Hu T'ung*, II, 551).

able.[147] Was not our master, then, a "ferry on the sea of suffering" and the "middle beam over the gate of the Law?" After he returned to his country and promulgated great wisdom, he skillfully persuaded and led the straying masses. His exposition of the doctrine transcends the past and present, and his name has become most famous. Had the master not been endowed with extraordinary talent[148] and blessed with the favors of both the Time and the Way, how could he have achieved such greatness? History does not relate his end; I therefore leave it unmentioned.

The eulogy says: Biographies differ concerning the day, month, and year of the Buddha's birth, and it is difficult to determine which is right. But Ŭiyŏn received the law from Fa-shang orally, and his calculation tallied with that in the *Pien-cheng lun* 辨正論 by Fa-lin 法琳 (572–640)[149] of T'ang. We should, therefore, follow it as our guide. But the renowned scholar O Se-mun 吳世文,[150] citing evidence from old documents, advanced a different opinion. Hence disputes arose. Although his thesis is detailed and his language beautiful, it is not sufficiently reliable.

---

147 A7al has 而 between 懸金 and 不刊. The translation of this passage is tentative.

148 A7a3 and *CPT*, I, 18, read 大拔 for 火拔.

149 For *Pien-cheng lun* see *T.* 52, 489c–550c, esp. 520c–522c. For his biography see *HKSC*, 24, 636b–639a, and *T.* 50, 198b–213b.

150 Is he the same man mentioned in *SGYS*, 3, 133, as a famous scholar and the author of the *Yŏktae ka* 歷代歌? The eldest of the three grandsons of O Hang-nin 吳學麟 (fl. 1171–1917), O Se-mun took the licentiate examination in the seventh month of 1152 (*KRS*, 74, 23a2). He was a friend of Yi Il-lo (*P'ahan chip*, p. 5) and Yi Kyu-bo (*Tongguk Yisangguk chip* [KKH], 5, 5a-15b; *Tongin sihwa* 東人詩話 [*CKK*, 1911], 1, 589). O Se-jae 吳世才, the youngest of the three, was one of the "Seven Sages of the Kangjwa" (*KRS*, 102, 3b, 10a–b).

Tamsi

Sŏk Tamsi 釋曇始[151] was a native of Kuan-chung 關中.[152] After becoming a monk he performed many miracles. [1017a] His feet were whiter than his face, and even when he was wading through mud they would not become wet. People called him the White-Footed Master. In the last year of the era *t'ai-yüan*[153] 大元 (396) of Chin, [Tamsi,] with several tens of scriptures and disciplinary texts, went to Liaotung to convert the people. Seizing favorable opportunities, he made known the principles of Buddhism, taught the Three Vehicles (*triyāna*),[154] and laid down the Triple Refuge and Five Commandments for the people.[155] The author of the *Liang kao-seng chuan* regards this as the beginning of Buddhism in Koguryŏ.[156] This was during the fifth year (395) of King Kwanggaet'o 廣開土王 (391–412),[157] the forty-first year of King Naemul (356–402)[158] of Silla, and the fifth year of King Asin 阿莘王 (392–405)[159] of Paekche, and was twenty-five years after Fu Chien of Ch'in sent over the scriptures and images of Buddha. Four years later, Fa-

---

151 In Wei Shou's *Shih-lao chih* he appears as Hui-shih 惠始; in *KSC*, 10, 392b, as T'an-shih 曇始. He came to Liaotung *ca.* 396. See Pak Yŏng-sŏn 朴永善, *Chosŏn sŏn'gyo ko*, 朝鮮禪教考 in *Zokuzōkyō*, IIB, 21/3, 269b.

152 The area between the Han and Lung passes, especially the area around Ch'ang-an.

153 For 大元 read 太元.

154 Which carry living beings across the sea of mortality to the shore of nirvāna: (1) *śrāvaka*, (2) *pratyeka-buddha*, (3) *Bodhisattva* (*Mahāyāna*). See P'yowŏn, *Hwaŏmgyŏng munŭi yogyŏl mundap*, 344a–348a.

155 歸戒: *triśarana* and *pañcaśila*. The former is the Triple Refuge (the Buddha, the Dharma, and the Order); the latter prohibits killing, stealing, adultery, lying, and the taking of strong drink. See Kim Tong-hwa (1), 14–15.

156 *KSC*, 10, 392b5–6. This is, of course, a Chinese view.

157 Nineteenth king of Koguryŏ. He became heir apparent of King Kogugyang in 386. During his reign he was known as Yŏngnak t'aewang 永樂太王. On the monument erected to commemorate his distinguished service to the state his full title is Kukkangsang kwanggaet'o kyŏngp'yŏngan hot'ae-wang 國岡上廣開土境平安好太王. See *SGSG*, 18, 4–5, and my *Studies in the Saenaennorae: Old Korean Poetry* (Rome, 1959), pp. 128–129, n. 21.

158 Seventeenth ruler of Silla, cousin and son-in-law of King Mich'u; his surname was Kim. He successfully repulsed the invasions of Japan (364) and Malgal 靺鞨. In 381 he sent an envoy to Fu Chien. *SGSG*, 3, 1–3.

159 Seventeenth ruler of Paekche, the eldest son of King Ch'imnyu; also called Abang 阿芳 or Ahwa 阿華. He often lost battles against Koguryŏ (394, 395, 396); in 397 he sent his son to Japan as a hostage; in 403 he attacked the Silla borders. *SGSG*, 25, 2–3.

hsien 法顯 (339–420)[160] went to India (399). Two years after Kumārajīva came to China (401), Master of the Law Hsüan-kao 玄高 (402–444)[161] was born.

In the beginning of the era *i-hsi* 義熙 (405–418) of Chin, Master Tamsi returned to Kuan-chung and began preaching in the Three Cities.[162] An uncle of Wang Hu 王胡, [163] a resident of Ch'ang-an, had been dead for several years. One day the uncle suddenly appeared [to Wang] in a dream and took him on a journey through Hell, showing him the various retributions suffered there. When the time for farewell came, the uncle said, "Now that you understand cause and effect, you should render respectful service to the monastery[164] of the White-Footed Master and cultivate good deeds." [Wang] Hu promised respectfully and awoke. He then inquired of all the monks; seeing Tamsi's feet whiter than his face, he attended him deferentially.

At the end of Chin, the Hsiung-nu Ho-lien Po-po 赫連勃勃 (381–407–425)[165] captured Kuan-chung and massacred innumerable people. The master was also attacked, but no blade could harm his person. After this, all the monks were pardoned, and none were killed. [Tamsi] escaped to the mountains and cultivated esoteric, ascetic practices. Not long afterwards, Ch'ang-an was recaptured by T'o-pa T'ao 拓拔燾 (408–424–451–452),[166] whose power spread over Kuan-chung and Lo-yang. At that time, Ts'ui Hao 崔浩 (381–450)[167] of Po-ling,[168] who had known Taoist magic from childhood, was

---

[160] He left for India in 399 and returned to Chien-k'ang in the fall of 413 (Frodsham, *Proceedings of the Second Biennial Congress*, p. 35, n. 35). His *Fa-kuo chi* 法國記 or *Fa-hsien hsing-chuan* 法顯行傳 was translated by Jean Rémusat (Paris, 1836), Klaproth and Landresse (Calcutta, 1848), Samuel Beal (London, 1869), James Legge (Oxford, 1886), and Herbert A. Giles (Cambridge, 1923). For his biography see *T.* 51, 857a–866c, and Adachi Kiroku 足立喜六, *Kōshō Hokken den* (Tokyo, 1936). *KSC*, 3, 337b–338b; *CSTCC*, 15, 111b–112b; *BD*, 526.

[161] *KSC*, 11, 397a–398b.

[162] Refers to the central part of modern Shensi.

[163] I cannot identify him.

[164] 阿練 *(araṇya) (HBGR*, pp. 34b–35a).

[165] Descendant of Ch'u P'i, king 右賢 of the Hsiung-nu. His father was Wei Ch'en 衞辰, who was killed by the Wei army. Po-po served under Yao Hsing of the Later Ch'in, but rebelled against him, called himself a descendant of Hsia, and styled himself "Heavenly Lord of Great Hsia." In 407 he established the state of Ta-hsia; in 413 he built the city of T'ung-wan. *Chin-shu*, 130, 1405b–1406d, and *Wei shu*, 95, 2106d–2107a (cf. *Wei shu*, 3, 1909a).

[166] *Wei shu*, 4A, 1909d–1912a.

[167] His *tzu* was Po-yüan 伯淵, a native of Ch'ing-ho, the eldest son of Ts'ui Hung, the *Li-pu shang-shu* of the Northern Wei. His biography is in *Wei shu*, 35, 1981a–1938c, and *Pei shih*, 21, 2811d–2814b; *BD*, 2035; *JAOS*, 53 (1933), 235 ff.

[168] For 傳陵 read 博陵, as in *KSC*, 10, 392b16; *SGYS*, 3, 125; and *CPT*, I, 12. The name of the

jealous of Buddhism. He was then minister of the new court and gained the confidence of T'ao. Together with the Taoist priest K'ou [Ch'ien-chih] 寇謙之 (d. 448),[169] he persuaded T'ao to outlaw Buddhism on the grounds that it did not benefit the world but instead injured the people's interests. T'ao, deluded by their words, issued a decree of annihilation in the seventh year of the era *t'ai-p'ing* 太平 (446). Soldiers were sent everywhere to burn down monasteries. Monks and nuns within the territory were forced to renounce their status. Those who attempted to escape were seized and killed, and their heads exposed.[170] As a result, not a single monk was left within the realm. Hsüan-kao and others were also killed at this time, the account of which is found in his biography. The master went to a place where soldiers could not reach him, and regretfully bided his time. At the end of the era *t'ai-p'ing* he calculated that the time for the conversion of T'ao was near. Therefore, on New Year's Day,[171] holding a metal staff in his hand,[172] he went to the palace gate.[173] The officer reported to the emperor that a white-footed monk was coming in right through the palace gate and that his appearance seemed strange. Hearing this, T'ao ordered strong soldiers to behead him, but to no avail. T'ao, in great anger, struck him with his sharp sword; but, except for the place struck by the weapon, which looked like the trace of a red thread, the master was completely unharmed.[174] T'ao then ordered him to be taken to the tigers' den in the Northern Park. The tigers, however, all lay sulking and would not approach him. But when T'ao ordered a Taoist priest to go near the den, [1017b] the animals roared and leapt toward him and were about to seize and devour him. From this T'ao realized that the power of Buddhism surpassed that of the Yellow Emperor and Lao Tzu;[175] he requested the master

town under the Later Wei corresponding to modern An-p'ing in Hopei and that under the Northern Chou to modern Lin-t'an in Kansu.

   169 Son of K'ou Hsiu-chih and brother of Ts'an-chih (363–448). For his biography see *Wei shu*, 42, 1995c, and *BD*, 984. See also Ch'en Yin-k'o, "Ts'ui Hao yü K'ou Ch'ien-chih," *Ling-nan hsüeh-pao* 嶺南學報, 11 (1950), 111–134; *JAOS*, 54 (1933), 225–239; Yang Lien-sheng, 17–38.

   170 See Tsukamoto Zenryū, *Shina bukkyōshi kenkyū: Hokugi hen* (Tokyo, 1942), pp. 99–130, and *Kōza bukkyō*, 4 (Tokyo, 1958), 131–142.

   171 *YSGYS*, p. 305, n. 1.

   172 金錫: "a monk's staff with resonant metal rings at the top."

   173 For 官門 read 宮門.

   174 This phrase is reminiscent of the description of the perfect sage in Taoism who neither injures the world nor is injured by it. Cf. *Nan-hua chen-ching*, 7, 56a (Giles, *Chuang Tzu*, p. 219).

   175 Maspero (4), p. 90, n. 1.

to go to his palace and there, bowing to his feet, repented his evil deeds.[176] The master explained the relentless truth of karma and, opening his palms, showed T'ao efficacious signs. T'ao was both ashamed and afraid, and [promised] to redeem the past and to do good in the future. But the evil he had done was irrevocable. As a result, T'ao fell ill; Ts'ui and K'ou also fell ill and were approaching death. Realizing that the disaster had been caused by these two, T'ao could not forgive their crime. He therefore destroyed the two families and proclaimed the restoration of Buddhism within his realm. Thus, the sounding of bells and chanting of hymns was resumed. When his grandson Hsün 濬 (440–452–465)[177] ascended the throne, he remembered the lesson[178] and promoted Buddhism. Thus, the precious system[179] rapidly came back to life. No one knows where the master finally went.

The eulogy says: When fire blazes over the K'un-lun Mountains,[180] gems and stones are scorched together. When frost lays waste the field, orchids *(lan)* and weeds die together.[181] The hardships and obstacles the master encountered were indeed extreme. The usual hardships of felling trees and removing their traces are far from providing an adequate comparison. Like a white cloud behind a green hill, he appeared and disappeared as occasion demanded. Like the moon's reflection on a deep pond, scooped out by a windlass,[182] he advanced and withdrew upon encountering dangers. He sacrificed

---

176 For 謽 as the old form of 您 see *Shuo wen* 說文 *(SPTK)*, 10B, 7b. See also n. 17 to the Introduction.

177 *Wei shu*, 5, 1914a–1915b.

178 深懲殷鑑: *Shih ching*, 255 (Karlgren, p. 216). Here "mirror" stands for the example of the downfall of the preceding dynasty.

179 This is my rendering of 寶氎制度. 氎 *(tieh, *d'iep)* is another graphic form of 疊 *(tieh)*, meaning "cotton." See Pelliot (8), pp. 442, 449, 453 *passim*, and *MBD*, II, 1077c–1078a.

180 火炎崑岡: *Shang shu*, 3, 14a (Legge, IV, 168).

181 蕭蘭共悴: Han Yü, *Ch'ang-li hsien-sheng chi* 昌黎先生集 *(SPPY)*, 1, 22b (Erwin von Zach, *Han Yü's Poetische Werke* [Cambridge, 1952], p. 18).

182 楒櫨, written also as 橁櫨, 轒轤 *(T. 54, 691a, 727a, and Tz'u t'ung* 辭通, 1, 73c–74a), is a "pulley," "windlass," or "winch." Perhaps Kakhun intends to say that a moon in the pond is disturbed temporarily by the pulley but remains basically intact; or he compares Tamsi's talent for protecting himself to the motion of a windlass, i.e., he ascends and descends, like a windlass, in order to avoid dangers; or, as the windlass cannot scoop out the reflected moon, so no danger was able to harm him. Or ". . . [Tamsi] waxed and waned like the reflections of the [bucket hanging from the] well-windlass in the deep blue well-water on moonlight nights," as Joseph Needham and Lu Gwei-Djen suggest. Lu and Needham add: "If one can see the bucket getting larger and larger reflected in the well-water as it descends, this is probably the image intended."

his body to save the drowned, and the Way flourished on this account. A Bodhisattva's protection of the Buddha-truth ought to be just like this. [The master] came to the country of the mulberry[183] and restored sight to those born blind. This must have been the fulfillment of his vows from a former life.

---

183 Does this refer to China? Or is it, like Fu-sang, a metaphor for "east" generally?

*Mālānanda

Sŏk Mālānanda 釋摩羅難陀[184] was from Serindia.[185] He was capable of
communicating with the supernatural, and there was no fathoming the precise
degree of his religious development. He traveled to all places, not confining
himself to one corner. According to the old records, he originally came to
China from India or Gandhāra. After that, he took the talented as his disciples
and by smoke of incense to attest the presence of the spirit, he attracted com-
panions.[186] He faced dangers undaunted and endured whatever hardships
came his way. As long as there were opportune conditions he sought them out,
regardless of the distance.

He came to this country from Chin in the ninth month of the ninth year
after the enthronement of the fourteenth king[187] of Paekche, Ch'imnyu
枕流王 (384).[188] The king went to greet him on the outskirts of the capital,
invited him and his entourage to the palace, deferred to him and worshiped
him, and listened respectfully to his sermon. With the court's favor en-
couraging them, the people were transformed. Buddhism thereafter spread
widely, and both king and subject esteemed it. The speed of its propagation
was as rapid as the transmission of royal orders by stages and couriers.[189]
In the second year (385), in the spring, a monastery was erected on Mount
Han 漢山[190] and ten monks were ordained in Mālānanda's honor. Buddhism

---

184 See n. 64 above.

185 For *hu* 胡 as referring to the languages of Serindia excluding Sanskrit and other Indian languages see T'ang Yung-t'ung, *Han-Wei liang-Chin Nan-pei-ch'ao fo-chiao-shih* 漢魏兩晉南北朝佛
教史 (Shanghai, 1938), I, 407.

186 The first phrase can be read as "Relying on materials, he metamorphosed himself." 烟 must
parallel 侶, alluding perhaps to the belief that the smoke of incense is able to make the devotees communicate with the Buddha, as in *T.* 40, 136b17 ff. and 54, 241b28–241c1. I owe this reference to
Professor Chow Tse-tsung of the University of Wisconsin.

187 Should be the first year of the fifteenth king, as in *SGYS*, 3, 121. *CPT*, I, 32, reads "the first
year of the fourteenth king, Ch'imnyu," which is wrong.

188 The eldest son of King Kŭn'gusu 近仇首王; succeeded his father in the seventh month (August
3–September 1) of 384; died in the eleventh month (December 18–January 16, 386) of 385. *SGSG*,
24, 7.

189 如置郵而傳命: *Mencius*, IIA, 1 (Legge, II, 184).

190 *SGSG*, 24, 7, reads: "in the second month of the second year." Hansan is modern Kwangju
廣州, on the lower reaches of the Han 漢. In 5 B.C. Onjo transferred his capital from Wiryesŏng 慰禮城

flourished in Paekche as it had done in Koguryŏ. Counting back to the year of Kāśyapa Mātaṅga's arrival in the Later Han, it had been more than 280 years.

The *Kiro ki* 耆老記[191] states that the ancestor of Koguryŏ, Chumong 朱蒙,[192] married a girl of Koguryŏ and had two sons, P'iryu 避流 and Ŭnjo 恩祖.[193] The two shared a common interest, went southward, and established a country in Hansan, the present Kwangju 廣州. The country was called Paekche[194] because at that time a hundred families came across the river.

to Hansan. King Kŭnch'ogo transferred the capital further south, to Namp'yŏngynagsŏng 南平壤城 (modern Seoul). In 475 the city fell into the hands of Koguryŏ. It acquired its present name in 940. *KRS*, 2, 13b; *KRSCY*, 1, 40a; *TYS*, 6, 5a–b.

191   Otherwise unknown.

192   Tongmyŏng 東明 (58–37–20–19 B.C.), founder of Koguryŏ. His surname was Ko 高, and his tabu names were Chumong, Ch'umo 鄒牟 (King Kwanggaet'o monument in *SGYS*, Appendix, p. 3), Sanghae 象解, Tomo 都慕 (*Shoku Nihongi* 續日本紀, in *Shintei zōho kokushi taikei*, II [Tokyo, 1937], 40, 546), and Tongmyŏng sŏngwang 東明聖王. His father was Kim Wa 金蛙, king of East Puyŏ 東夫餘, and his mother, Yu Hwa 柳花, daughter of Habaek 河伯. According to *SGSG*, 12, 1–2, upon the death of Haeburu 解夫婁, king of East Puyŏ, Kim Wa ascended the throne, setting up Yu Hwa as his wife. When he heard that she had had relations with Haemosu 解慕漱, son of the Heavenly God, he imprisoned her in a dark chamber. There she received a ray of sunlight, became pregnant, and gave birth to an egg, from which came a male child. He grew up and called himself Chumong. Of the seven sons of Kim, all were inferior in talent to Chumong; and in spite of the king's opposition the brothers plotted to kill him. Chumong escaped and set up his court at Cholbon 卒本, making his kingdom Koguryŏ and using Ko as his surname. In 34 B.C. he constructed walled cities and palaces; in 32 B.C. he destroyed the country of Haengin 荇人國; in 27 B.C. he absorbed North Okchŏ. The legends connected with his birth and life have been a favorite subject of study. As early as the first century, the author of the *Lun heng*, 2, 16a–b (Forke, I, 175), made reference to his extraordinary birth. Yi Kyu-bo wrote a long poem on the king which is preserved in the *Tongguk Yisangguk chip*, 3, 1a–9a. In an article published in the *Naitō hakushi shōju kinen shigaku ronsō* 內藤博士頌壽記念史學論叢 (Tokyo, 1930), pp. 715–741, Imanishi Ryū compares the legend of Chumong with several similar stories orally transmitted in northeastern Korea concerning the birth of a Manchurian chieftain and often referring to Nurhachi (1559–1626). See also Shiratori Kurakichi 白鳥庫吉, "The Legend of the King Tung-ming, the Founder of the Fu-yu-kuo," *MTB*, 10 (1938), 1–39, which is a translation of his article first printed in the *Hattori sensei koki shukuga kinen ronbunshū* 服部先生古稀祝賀記念論文集 (Tokyo, 1936), pp. 537–570; *TG*, 28 (1941), 169–189; *Sŏnggyun'gwan taehakkyo nonmunjip*, 7 (1962), 84–117. For a résumé of previous studies on the subject by Naitō, Mishina, Imanishi, and Shiratori, see Mitamura Taisuke's 三田村泰助 article in the *Ritsumeikan bungaku* 立命館文學, 70–72 (1949), 97–117, where the author opts for Mishina's interpretation and proposes that the Chumong legend is characteristic of the foundation myths of the Tungusic people. For the king's tomb inscriptions (1892) see *CKS*, nos. 522, 523, 524. *SGYS*, 1, 41, repeats the account in *Wei shu*, 100, 2123a, and in *Tongguk Yisangguk chip*, 3, 5a, and proposes that Chumong means "a good archer."

193   Yang, p. 161, reads *onje* as "a hundred generations" or "entire period". See *Han'guk sa*, I, 337 ff.

194   Also written as 伯濟, 慰禮城, and 百殘 (on the monument to King Kwanggaet'o). Yang, pp. 141, 156–157, reads it *palkchat* or *palchae* ("a city of light"). Here our author is referring to the forced etymology invented by the compilers of the *Sui shu*, 81, 2532a39 (cf. *SGSG*, 37, 4). *SGYS*,

Later, the two set up their own states, separately, around Kongju 公州[195] in Puyŏ County 扶餘郡.

In the sea to the southeast of Three Han is the land of Wae 倭 (that is, Japan). [1019c] To the northeast of Wae is the Country of the Hairy Man 毛人國.[196] To the northeast of the latter is the Country of the Tattooed Body 文身國,[197] two thousand leagues east of which lies Great Han, while twenty thousand leagues east of the latter lies Fu-sang 扶桑.[198] Five Indian monks arrived there [that is, in Japan] during the Sung and only then did Buddhism begin to prosper. These countries were all in the sea. From time to time monks from Wae traveled across the sea, but [whether from] the rest is unknown.

The so-called Three Han were Mahan 馬韓, Pyŏnhan 弁韓, and Chinhan

---

2, 96–97, advances another story: Onjo established his capital in Hanam Wiryesŏng (modern Kwang-ju?) and had ten ministers assist him in the administration of the country. Hence the country was called Sipche 十濟. *CPT*, I, 32, reads 濟河 for 渡—.

195 Ungch'ŏn 熊川 of Paekche. In 475 Paekche transferred its capital from Pukhansansŏng 北漢山城 to Ungch'ŏn, and in 538 farther south to Puyŏ 扶餘 (*SGSG*, 37, 4). In 660 T'ang established the Hsiung-ch'uan tu-hu-fu 熊川都護府 (*TYS*, 17, 10a); from 670 on, it fell under Silla control. The city acquired the present name in 940 (*KRS*, 56, 26b–27a; *TYS*, 17, 1a–b).

196 *Shan-hai ching* 山海經 (*SPTK*), 9, 48a, and *Index du Chan Hai King* (Peiping, 1948), p. 41.

197 According to *Nan shih*, 79, 2732c (*Liang shu*, 54, 1842a, has the same account), the country is "7,000 *li* northeast of Japan. Its people have stripes on their bodies like those of an animal and have three lines on their foreheads. Those whose lines are straight are noble, while those whose lines are small are base. They are a joy-loving people. Their products are abundant and cheap; travelers need not carry provisions. There are houses, but not walled cities. The king's palace is decorated with gold, silver, and jewels. Around the house there is a ditch, ten feet wide, into which mercury is poured. Rain falls on the mercury. In transactions jewelry is used. A criminal of light offense is beaten by a club, while sentenced criminals are devoured by wild animals. If the criminal is innocent, the animal will not eat him. After a night's confinement, he is then released and pardoned." Gustaaf Schlegel, in "Wen-chin Kouo," *TP*, A3 (1892) 490–494, identifies it with the Kuriles. *CPT*, I, 32, omits "to the northeast of the latter."

198 *Nan shih*, 79, 2732c-d; Schlegel, in *TP*, A3 (1892), 114–168; A5 (1894), 291–298; A6 (1895), 85–92, identifies it with Sakhalin (Ainu). See also Bertold Laufer, "Optical Lenses," *TP*, 16 (1915), 198–200. Sugimoto Naojirō 杉本直治郎 and Mitarai Masaru 御手洗勝, in their article in *Minzoku-gaku kenkyū* 民族學研究, 15 (1950), 304–327, suggest that the Fu-sang legend was originally a "pure sun-legend" and that its place of origin was the Shantung peninsula, where the cult of sun worship was practiced during the Chou period. They conclude that the meaning of the term was "the place where the sun rises." Katō Jōken 加藤常賢, on the other hand, elaborates further on this theory and proposes that Fu-sang was synonymous with 巨商 and 暘谷, "a female organ which gave birth to the sun." The Japanese of the time of Prince Shōtoku believed that the sun rose in their country and adopt-ed the name to refer to their land (*SZ*, 60 [1951], 617–626). In *SGYS*, 3, 126, the term is used to refer generally to the East.

辰韓.[199] The *Pao-tsang ching* 寶藏經[200] records that in the northeast there is the country of Chindan 震旦, also called China 支那 (*Cīna*). Its name means "full of thoughts,"[201] for the people of the country used to ponder over things. This, then, was the country of Great T'ang. But the Three Han were in the northeast of Jambudvīpa and were not islands. They came into being 600 years after Buddha had entered nirvāṇa. In the middle rises Mount Sŏngju 聖住山, called *Śrīmudrā* 室利母恒梨.[202] High and steep, on its summit, Mount Moon 月岳,[203] is a palace of the Bodhisattva Avalokiteśvara.[204] It is difficult to write about the sacred place in detail. Paekche was another name for Mahan.

The *Sung kao-seng chuan* says that [Mālā] nanda had attained samādhi[205]

---

199 For Yang's reading of these terms as *saenham, mahan,* and *karahan* respectively see pp. 151–152.

200 He may be referring to the *Tsa pao-tsang ching* 雜寶藏經 (*T.* 4, 447a-499a), translated by Kinkara and T'an-yao in 472 in 10 chapters. Or more likely to the *Pao-tsang lun* (*T.* 45, n. 1857) by Seng-chao in 3 chapters. The work is entered in the *I-wen chih* of *Sung shih,* 205, 4995c18, and Ŭich'ŏn's catalogue (*T.* 55, 1177c). The work was imported into Japan in 858. Tsukamoto Zenryū, *ed., Jōron kenkyū* 肇論研究 (Kyoto, 1955), pp. 149, 274–275.

201 *Cintanā* in Sanskrit means "thought." Hence this is a folk etymology without any historical basis, as pointed out by Matsumoto Bunsaburō 松本文三郎 in *SR,* 12 (1927), 45. See also *T.* 54, 447c and 939b, and n. 31 above.

202 Kakhun's gloss reads: "In Chinese, 'Three Seal Mountain' "; this I cannot identify. Perhaps *śrī* and *tri* are confused.

203 According to *TYS,* 14, 4a-b, and *Taedong unbu kunok,* 18, 37b, there is a mountain with the same name 45 *ri* east of Ch'ungju 忠州 and 50 *ri* south of Ch'ŏngp'ung 清風, North Ch'ungch'ŏng. It was called Wŏrhyŏng mountain during Silla and there is a monastery called Wŏrak (*TYS,* 14, 19a).

204 These passages are curiously reminiscent of those in *T.* 51, 175b21–24 (cf. *T.* 9, 589c–590a) which describe the sacred place of Mañjuśrī. As the northeast is the direction in which Mañjuśrī is said to reside on Mount Ch'ing-liang (*TP,* 48 [1960], 83), so Kakhun, perhaps out of Buddhist piety and nationalism, is attempting to create a myth that Avalokiteśvara resides in the northeast, on Wŏrak in Korea. Like Mount Potolaka in South India, P'u-t'o shan 普陀山, an island off the coast of Ningpo, is a sacred place of Avalokiteśvara to the Chinese (*Tu-shih fang-yü chi-yao* [*WYWK*], 92, 3867; *HJAS,* 8 [1944], 174, n. 160). This may also have given Kakhun a clue. Mount Nak in Kangwŏn Province is, of course, named after Potolaka (*SGYS,* 3, 159). Mishina Shōei points out a certain affinity between the cult of Avalokiteśvara in Silla and Koryŏ and popular beliefs, especially the belief in a fertility goddess in Korea. He then cites, as examples, the story of Avalokiteśvara on Mount Nak and the fertility goddess, mother of Chumong, of Koguryŏ. See *Bukkyō shigaku,* 4 (1954), 25–27.

205 This quotation is in *SKSC,* 20, 837c27–28. That one "could enter the water and not get wet, could enter the fire and not get burned" is attributed in *Mou tzu* 牟子 to a Buddha (Pelliot [6], 292) and in *Chuang tzu* to the true man of old or the man of perfect virtue (*Nan-hua chen-ching* 3, 2b [Watson, *Chuang Tzu,* p. 73], and 6, 20b–21a [Watson, p. 104]). For *samādhi* ("concentration" or "trance") see *BHSD,* pp. 568b-569a, and Har Dayal, *The Bodhisattva Doctrine in Buddhist Sanskrit Literature* (London, 1932), pp. 221 ff.

and that he did not get wet in water or burned by fire. He could transform stones into gold, and his manifestations were endless. This occurred during the era *chien-chung* 建中[206] The two dates are far apart; this might not be the same monk.

The eulogy says: The masses, generally ignorant and rebellious by nature, disobey some royal decrees or court orders. But once they hear about miracles or see wonders, they reform their personalities, shift to the good, cultivate the genuine, and face towards the inside [of their characters], because they are following what is opportune.[207] It is indeed true that good words can evoke a response from more than a thousand leagues away.[208] The way to grasp opportunities, however, lies in seizing an appropriate moment. Therefore, the monk's efforts were half [those] of the ancients; his achievements, however, were twice theirs.[209]

---

206 The chronology is uncertain. *Chien-chung* is a reign title of T'ang Te-tsung (780-783) as well as of Sung Hui-tsung (1101–1102). For 拒 read 距, as in *CPT*, I, 33.

207 My version of 革面遷善, 修眞面內 follows the suggestions of Professors Chow and Robinson.

208 出其言善則千里之外應: *Chou i*, 7, 5b (Wilhelm, I, 328).

209 故事半古(之)人功必倍之: *Mencius*, IIA, 1 (Legge, II, 184–185).

Ado

Sŏk Ado 釋阿道[210] is said to have been a native of India. Some say he came from Wu, while others hold that he went first to Wei from Koguryŏ and returned to Silla. We do not know which is correct.[211]

He was distinguished in manner and appearance, and his miracles were most strange.[212] He held it his duty to travel and convert, and wondrous flowers rained from Heaven whenever he preached. At first, during the reign of King Nulchi 訥祗王 (417–458) of Silla, Hŭkhoja 黑胡子[213] arrived in Ilsŏn County from Koguryŏ to enlighten those who had the appropriate karma. Morye 毛禮,[214] a resident of the county, prepared a secret chamber[215] in his home to receive him. At that time, [the state of] Liang (502–557) dispatched an envoy with gifts of garments and incense;[216] but neither the king nor his officials knew the name or use of the incense. The king's messenger [there-

---

210 His name is also written as 我道 (*SGYS*, 3, 122) or 阿頭 (*SGYS*, 3, 121, 122) (cf. Yang, p. 203). According to *Ado hwasang sajŏk pi* 阿道和尙 事蹟碑 (erected in 1639) in *CJS*, I, 424–426, and *CKS*, II, 876–877, his father, A Kulma 阿堀摩 (我—— in *SGYS*, 3, 122, and *CJS*, I, 356, and 阿——in *CJS*, I, 424), came to Koguryŏ in 356, and Ado, born in 357, went at the age of sixteen to Wei to see his father (372) and returned at the age of nineteen to his mother (375). I have not yet been able to determine which sources the builders of this monument used to obtain such precise dates. *Ado hwasang pi*, in *CKS*, I, 25, does not pretend to such accuracy. Eda Shunyū, in *Bunka*, 2 (1935), 967, claims that A Kulma was from Serindia, without, of course, any documentation. Some still advance such an untenable folk etymology as that the name Ado came from 児道/頭 (*Pulgyo hakpo*, 2 [1964], 305, n. 7). There is, however, no similarity between the sounds 阿 (**â*) and 児 (**niĕg*).

211 *SGYS*, 3, 122, asserts that he was from Koguryŏ. See n. 29 to the Introduction.

212 A10b7 and *CPT*, I, 7, read 尤奇 for 左-.

213 The first logograph in his name is often written as 墨 (e.g., *SGYS*, 3, 122). Although there is little evidence to suggest that he was from Serindia, his name bespeaks a foreign origin. As Tao-an (312–385), because of his dark complexion, was called "the dark one" 崑崙子, so Muk (Hŭk) hoja was called a "dark Serindian" because of his foreign traits, especially his unusually dark complexion (*SGYS*, 3, 124). For Tao-an's case see *TP*, 46 (1958), 9–10, n. 1.

214 Or Morok 毛祿 (*SGYS*, 3, 122). An interesting reading and meaning is advanced by Eda Shunyū in *Bunka*, 2 (1935), 984, and *Kōza bukkyō*, 4 (1958), 257, where he reads Morye as *Torure* (*T'ŏllye* in Korean) and suggests that the Japanese word *tera* and the Korean word *chŏl* ("monastery") derive from his name (repeated in the *Japanese-English Buddhist Dictionary* [Tokyo, 1965], p. 318a). Eda also thinks that Morye, like Soga in Fujiwara Japan, is a clan name and that there must have been a small Buddhist community (*Bunka*, 2, 971).

215 窟室: *Tso chuan*, Duke Hsiang 30 (Legge, V, 557a). *SGYS*, 3, 122, reads 堀 for 窟.

216 That Liang is impossible chronologically has been pointed out in *SGYS*, 3, 122.

fore] was sent out with the incense to make inquiries [concerning it] both inside and outside the country. Once [Hŭk] hoja saw it, he disclosed its name, saying, "When burnt, it emits a sweet fragrance [1018a] which will carry one's devotion to the gods and spirits. The title 'sacred'[217] belongs to nothing other than the Three Jewels *(triratna)*—the Buddha, the Dharma, and the Order. If one burns this incense and makes a vow, a response is sure to follow." At that time the illness of the king's daughter took a turn for the worse, and the king ordered [Hŭk] hoja to burn the incense and make a vow. The princess soon recovered. The king rejoiced and rewarded him amply. [Hŭk] hoja returned to Morye, and, after giving him all that he had received from the king, said, "I have a place to go; hence I wish to bid you farewell." After that no one knew where he went.[218]

In the time of King Pich'ŏ (479–500),[219] Master *(Upādhyāya)* Ado, together with three attendants, also came to the house of Morye. His appearance was similar to that of [Hŭk] hoja. After several years, he died a natural death. The three attendants remained reciting *sūtra* and *vinaya*, and occasionally some became converted and practiced the faith.

Yet, according to the old records, on the eleventh day of the third month of the first year of the era *ta-t'ung* of Liang, Ado came to Ilsŏn County,[220] and both Heaven and Earth trembled. The master, holding a metal staff with gold rings in his left hand and uplifting a jade vessel of supreme response[221] in his right, wearing a colorful cassock, and reciting a revealed truth,[222] came to the believer Morye's house. [Mo]rye, surprised and fearful, went out to meet him and said, "Formerly, when the Ko[gu]ryŏ monk Chŏngbang[223] 正方 came to our country, the king and officials regarded his advent as an evil omen and killed him. Another [monk], named Myŏlgubi 滅垢玭,[224]

217 A11a2 reads 神聖 for 神靈, which is correct.

218 The above is not in *SGYS*, 3, 122.

219 Twenty-first king of Silla, also called Choji 照知; the eldest son of King Chabi (458–479). *SGSG*, 3, 7–9; *SGYS*, 3, 123–124.

220 See n. 29 to the Introduction.

221 玉鉢應器: A spiritually responsive bowl, a bowl sensitive to supernatural presences, an instrument of divination, miraculously created.

222 花詮: the same term occurs in the second line of a four-line, seven-word verse written by Ŭich'ŏn after a lecture on T'ien-t'ai at the Kukch'ŏng monastery in 1100 (*Taegak kuksa munjip*, 20, 4b2).

223 Otherwise unknown.

224 Otherwise unknown.

came after him, and he too was killed. What are you seeking that you should come here? Please come in quickly, lest you be seen by the neighbors.'' He then took the monk to a secret room and served him with diligence. It happened, then, that an envoy from the Wu presented five kinds of incense to King Wŏnjong 原宗王 (514–540).[225] The king did not know their use, and asked the people in the country. When the messenger came to the master, the master told him that they were things to be burned to serve the Buddha. Afterward he went to the capital with the messenger, and the king asked him to meet the [Wu] envoy. The envoy paid him great respect, saying, ''Eminent monks are no strangers in this remote country after all.'' The king learned through this that the Buddha and his order were to be venerated, and issued a decree permitting the propagation [of Buddhism].

According to the *Sisa* 詩史[226] by Ko Tŭk-sang 高得相, the Liang sent an envoy, Yüan-piao 元表,[227] who presented rosewood incense,[228] scriptures, and images of Buddha. Because no one knew their use, the king made inquiries in all four directions, and Ado took the opportunity to point out the Law. [Ko Tŭk-]sang comments that Ado twice encountered danger of death, but that thanks to his supernatural power *(abhijñā)* he did not die but took refuge in the home of Morye. Thus, whether the envoy came from Liang or Wu cannot be ascertained. The life of Ado was, morever, similar to that of Hŭkhoja. But why is this so? A span of some 410 years separates the era *yung-p'ing* 永平 from the year *chŏngmi* 丁未 of the era *ta-t'ung* (527). Buddhism had been in existence in Koguryŏ for more than 150 years, and in Paekche for more than 140 years.

According to another story, in the *Sui chŏn* 殊異傳[229] by Pak Il-lyang

---

225 In *Liang shu*, 54, 1841d, and *Nan shih*, 79, 2732b, he appears as 募泰; in *Ts'e-fu yüan-kuei* 冊府元龜 (Chung-hua shu-chü ed.), 996, 4a, as 募秦. Yang reads his temple name as *Ch'almara* (p. 230). *SGSG*, 4, 2–4.

226 詠史詩 in *SGYS*, 3, 122. Ko Tŭk-sang appears in the *I-wen chih* of *Sung shih*, 203, 4992a (Suematsu, *Shiragi-shi no shomondai*, p. 223).

227 Otherwise unknown. *SKSC*, 30, 895b-c (*CPT*, III, 206; *SGYS*, 3, 122), however, lists another monk with the same name, a Silla national who went to T'ang and Serindia in the middle of the eighth century.

228 湛檀 in *SGYS*, 3, 122. For *abhijñā*, a few lines below, see n. 448.

229 *SGYS*, 3, 122, cites the *Ado ponbi* 阿道本碑 as its source (cf. *CKS*, I, 25). *Sui chŏn* is also known as *Silla ijŏn* 新羅異傳 (*SGYS*. 4, 187) or *Silla sui chŏn*. It is a collection of tales in the *ch'uan-ch'i* tradition. The book itself is long lost, but at least thirteen stories survive in quotations preserved in eight works, the earliest of which is *HKC*. It used to be attributed to Ch'oe Ch'i-wŏn or Pak Il-lyang;

朴寅亮 (1047–1096),[230] the master's father was a native of Wei, named Kulma 崛摩, and his mother a native of Ko[gu]ryŏ, named Ko To-nyŏng 高道寧. During Kulma's stay in Koguryŏ in an official capacity, he had an affair [with Ko To-nyŏng]. Later he returned to Wei, leaving her pregnant. When the master reached the age of five, he had a wondrous appearance. [1018b] His mother told him, "You are an unfavored orphan, so you had better become a monk." The master followed her advice, and on that very day shaved his head. At sixteen, he went to Wei to visit Kulma and there studied under the master (*Upādhyāya*) Hsüan-chang 玄彰.[231] Nineteen years after ordination,[232] he returned to his mother, who told him: "It is very difficult to promote the Law in this country, for conditions are not yet ripe. Although at this moment there is no oral transmission of the doctrine in that land of Silla, three thousand months from now[233] an enlightened king, a protector of the Law, shall hold sway and greatly advance the Buddha's cause. In the capital, there are seven places where the Law shall abide: Ch'ŏn'gyŏngnim 天鏡林 ("Forest of the Heavenly Mirror"), east of Kŭmgyo 金橋 (the present Hŭngnyun monastery 興輪寺);[234] Samch'ŏn'gi 三川岐 (the present Yŏnghŭng monastery 永興寺);[235] south of the Dragon Palace 龍宮南 (the

---

Ch'oe Kang-hyŏn studied the authorship and contents of the book and concludes that the real author of this collection is Kim Ch'ŏng-myŏng 金陟明 (*fl.* 1010–1083; *SGYS*, 4, 184). See Ch'oe's article in *Kugŏ kungmunhak*, 25 (1962), 147–163, and 26 (1963), 89–106.

230 Hallim academician, statesman, and writer, Pak flourished under Kings Munjong and Sukchong 肅宗 of Koryŏ. When a boundary dispute arose between Liao and Koryo, his memorial was enough to pacify the Liao sovereign, who abandoned his claim (1075). On another occasion (1080) he accompanied the envoy Yu Hong 柳洪 (d. 1091) to Sung; when their ship was wrecked near Chekiang the party escaped, but the tribute they were carrying was lost. It was only through Pak's diplomacy that the party escaped punishment. Pak's reputation as a poet was so high that the Sung Chinese published some of his poems in the anthology called *Hsiao-hua chi* (*Sohwa chip* 小華集). This work includes the poetry of his friend Kim Kun. In his later years he served as Left Executive of the Department of Ministries and Second Privy Councilor (*Ch'amji chŏngsa* 參知政事). His collected works, *Kogŭm nok* 古今錄, were compiled first in 1284 and re-edited in 1357. For his biography see *KRS*, 95, 17b–18b (11, 9b). See also *CMP*, 244, 4a; 247, 2a–b, and *KS*, 463a–464a and 855a.

231 I cannot identify him. *CKS*, II, 876, has 玄暢. Professor Arthur F. Wright informs me that there are two Hsüan-ch'ang dating from the fifth century.

232 *SGYS*, 3, 122, and *CJS*, I, 424, read "at nineteen," which is difficult to believe.

233 In the original, "thirty." Should read 3,000, as in *SGYS*, 3, 122.

234 Situated east of Kŭmgyo 金橋, also called Sŏch'ŏn'gyo 西川橋. The construction was begun in 527 and completed in 544 (*SGSG*, 4, 4). It is two *ri* south of Kyŏngju (*TYS*, 21, 30b). For the tiles and bricks excavated near the site of the monastery see *Kogo misul* 考古美術, no. 59 (June 1965), 17–21. Cf. *SGYS*, 3, 123. For 與 read 興, as in A12b2.

235 Constructed at exactly the same time as the above (*SGYS*, 3, 123; *TYS*. 21. 30b).

present Hwangnyong monastery 皇龍寺);[236] north of the Dragon Palace (the present Punhwang monastery 芬皇寺);[237] Sinyu Forest 神遊林 (the present Ch'ŏnwang monastery 天王寺);[238] Sach'ŏnmi 沙川尾 (the present Yŏngmyo monastery 靈妙寺);[239] and the Sŏch'ŏng Field 婿請田 (the present Tamŏm monastery 曇嚴寺.[240] At these places are ruins of monasteries *(saṅghārāma)* built during the time of the former Buddha, which escaped earlier destruction. You should go there, proclaim the mysterious doctrine, and become the founder of Buddhism. Would that not be wonderful?"

In the second year, *kyemi* 癸未 (263), of King Mich'u (262–284),[241] the master, obeying his mother's instructions, went to live in Silla, west of the palace (the present Ŏmjang monastery 嚴莊寺). When he asked permission to preach, some thought it strange because this [practice] was hitherto unknown, and some even attempted to kill him. He therefore escaped to the village of Sok 續村, the present Sŏnju 善州,[242] and hid in the house of Morok for three years. It happened then that Princess Sŏngguk 成國公主 was ill, and the king sent out messengers everywhere for a healer. The master answered the call, went to the palace, and cured the princess' illness. Overjoyed, the king asked him what he desired. The master replied, "If you will build a monastery in the Forest of the Heavenly Mirror, I shall be well content." The king complied. But the age was crude, the people were stubborn, and it

---

236 The construction was begun in the second month (March 1–29) of 553 and temporarily finished in the second month of 566 (*SGSG*, 4, 5 and 6; *TYS*, 21, 30a-b); it was finally completed in 645.

237 Situated five *ri* east of Kyŏngju; it was completed in the first month (February 4–March 4) of 634. *SGSG*, 5, 1; *TYS*, 21, 18a.

238 Located on the southern slope of Mount Nang, nine *ri* east of Kyŏngju, it was completed during the eighth month (September 11-October 9) of 679. *SGSG*, 7, 10; *TYS*, 21, 7a, 30b. In *SGYS*, 3, 123 and 124, Sach'ŏnmi comes first as no. 5.

239 Five *ri* west of Kyŏngju. The monastery was completed in 635 (*SGSG*, 5, 1; *TYS*, 21, 18a). It was damaged by fire in 662, 666, 668, and 703 (*SGSG*, 6, 3, 5, and 7). See also *SGSG*, 32, 2, and 38, 4, where it is written 廟 throughout. For the proving of the site of the monastery see *Kogo misul*, no. 23 (June 1962), 5–10.

240 *TYS*, 21, 29b, has no description of it.

241 For 末 read 未, as in *SGYS*, 3, 123.

242 *SGYS*, 3, 123, has 續林. Modern Sŏnsan, 536 *ri* south of Seoul. According to *TYS*, 29, 8a, and *CJS*, I, 424–426, the former residence of Ado on Mount Naeng 冷山, 15 *ri* east of Sŏnsan, was called the Tori monastery 桃李寺 because of the following story: When Ado came to Morye's house and sat in meditation, brilliant light flooded the room, its brightness spreading to Heaven and Earth. Morye went out in surprise, climbed the hill at the back, and found a most wonderful place for a hermitage. There he built one; the peach trees then started to blossom amid the snow. He therefore named the hermitage Tori, and the village beneath it Togae 桃開.

was difficult to make converts. The master at this time used a humble hut as his monastery. Only after seven years were there some who desired to be ordained as monks. Morok's sister, Sashi 史侍,[243] became a nun. Therefore, the Yŏnghŭng monastery was erected at Samch'ŏn'gi where she stayed. After King Mich'u died, his successor did not respect Buddhism and wanted to proscribe it. The master returned to the village of Sok and made a grave for himself. He entered the grave, closed the slab over himself, and died. The sacred religion, therefore, was not practiced in Silla 斯盧.[244] Two hundred years later, King Wŏnjong finally propagated Buddhism.[245] This happened just as To-nyŏng had predicted. But from King Mich'u to King Pŏphŭng there were eleven kings. What a discrepancy concerning the dates of Ado's life! Old records must be scrutinized carefully. If Buddhism was practiced under King Mich'u, the master must have been a contemporary of Sundo.[246] In that case, the faith underwent a decline and revived during the era *ta-t'ung* of Liang. Hŭkhoja and Yüan-piao, by this reckoning, appeared together, and therefore their careers are described here for the reader's inspection.

[1018c] The eulogy says: When Buddhism spread eastward, although the fight between the faithful and blasphemous never ceased, the beginning was auspicious and each generation had its promoters. Take, for example, Ado and Hŭkhoja. They hid and appeared at will, possessing the characterless (*alakṣaṇa*) Dharma-body (*Dharmakāya*). One before and one after, they seemed to be two different persons;[247] but one cannot decide everything about their lives, for one cannot catch the wind or grasp a reflection.[248] But both tried their plans first before carrying out the work of propagation. In the biginning they met dangers, but escaped them and finally achieved success. Even Li-fang of Ch'in or [Kāśyapa] Mātaṅga of Han could not surpass them.

---

243 史氏 in *SGYS*, 3, 123. We should remember that the queen of King Pŏphŭng emulated her example and became a nun.

244 *SGSG*, 34, 1, lists a number of different transcriptions for Silla (*SGSG*, 4, 1); in *Wei chih*, 30, 1005d, entered as Saro.

245 For 像(象) 教(法), which is a rendering of Sanskrit *pratirūpaka dharma*, see Pelliot (7) and *TP*, 15 (1915), 472.

246 This chronology is impossible. How could Sundo, who came to Koguryŏ in 372, be a contemporary of Ado if Ado came during the latter part of the third century?

247 For 似同異 read 似同似異 with *CPT*, I, 10.

248 捕風搏影: *Wei Chiang-chou chi* 韋江州集 (*SPTK*), 10, 5b.

The *Book of Changes* says: "[The superior man] contains the means in his own person. He bides his time and then acts."[249] This is a good footnote to Ado.

---

[249] 藏器待時 alludes to 君子藏器干身待時而動 in *Chou i*, 8, 4b (Wilhelm, I, 364).

Pŏpkong

Sŏk Pŏpkong was the twenty-third king of Silla, Pŏphŭng (514–540). His secular name was Wŏnjong 原宗; he was the first son of King Chijŭng 智證王 (500–514)[250] and Lady Yŏnje 延帝夫人. He was seven feet tall. Generous, he loved the people, and they [in turn] regarded him as a saint or a sage. Millions of people, therefore, placed confidence in him.[251] In the third year (516) a dragon appeared in the Willow Well 楊井.[252] In the fourth year (517)[253] the Board of War was established, and in the seventh year (520) laws and statutes were promulgated together with the official costumes.[254] After his enthronement, whenever the king attempted to spread Buddhism, his ministers opposed him with much dispute.[255] He felt frustrated, but, remembering Ado's devout vow, he summoned all his officials and said to them: "Our august ancestor, [King] Mich'u, together with Ado, propagated Buddhism, but he died before great merits were accumulated. That the knowledge of the wonderful transformation of Śākyamuni[256] should be prevented from spreading makes me very sad. We think we ought to erect monasteries and

---

250 Son of King Kalmun. In 503 he established the name of the kingdom as Silla. His posthumous title is Chijŭng; he was the first Silla king to receive such a title. His tabu names were Chidaero 智大路, Chidoro 智度路, and Chich'ŏllo 智哲老 (*SGSG*, 4, 1–2).

251 彰信兆民: *Shang shu*, 4, 3b (Legge, III, 180).

252 *SGSG*, 4, 2, reads 楊山井中. Kwŏn Sang-no 權相老 (1879–1965), in an article in the *Pulgyo hakpo* 佛教學報, 1 (1963), 81–108, deals with the belief in the dragon among the Paekche and Silla people. The dragon cult seems to have had its origins first in autochthonous beliefs and later in Buddhism. The use of the logograph "dragon" in the names of mountains, rivers, temples, and villages reflects the extent of the popularization of this cult. Another suggestion offered by Kwŏn is that of the development of the dragon cult into the Maitreya cult in Silla. The belief in the power and virtue of the dragon king somehow coalesced with that in Maitreya as a Bodhisattva residing in the Tuṣita Heaven and as the future Buddha on earth. Kwŏn points out that even the native words for dragon, *miru* and *miri* (Yu Ch'ang-don 劉昌惇, *Yijoŏ sajŏn* 李朝語辭典 [Seoul, 1964], pp. 345–346), are similar in sound to the word for Maitreya, *Mirŭk*.

253 *SGSG*, 4, 2, has the fourth month (May 6-June 4) of the fourth year. *SGSG*, 38, 2, has the third year (516).

254 朱紫: in T'ang times, those above the fifth grade wore red and purple robes; hence figuratively used to mean "high officials" or "nobles."

255 *CPT*, I, 48, reads 喋喋; *Pulgyo*, 23 (April 1940), 27, reads 喋喋.

256 For 能仁 or 能儒 as referring to Śākyamuni see Tsukamoto, pp. 121–122, n. 1, and *HBGR*, pp. 190a-197b.

recast images to continue our ancestor's fervor. What do you think?'' Minister Kongal 恭謁[257] and others remonstrated with the king, saying, "In recent years the crops have been scarce,and the people are restless.[258] Besides, because of frequent border raids from the neighboring state, our soldiers are still engaged in battle. How can we exhort our people to erect a useless building at this time?'' The king, depressed at the lack of faith among his subordinates, sighed, saying, "We,[259] lacking moral power, are unworthy of succeeding to the throne. The *yin* and the *yang* are disharmonious and the people[260] ill at ease; therefore you opposed my idea and did not want to follow. Who can enlighten the strayed people by the wonderful Law?'' For some time no one answered.

In the sixteenth year (529)[261] the Grand Secretary (*Naesa sain* 內史舍人)[262] Pak Yŏmch'ok 朴厭髑 (Ich'adon 異次頓 or Kŏch'adon 居次頓),[263] then twenty-six years old, was an upright man. With a heart that was sincere

---

[257] 工目 or 謁恭 in *SGYS*, 3, 126; otherwise unknown.

[258] This is a fabrication. *SGSG* does not record any famine or flood in the beginning of his reign.

[259] 寡人: *Li chi* 禮記 (*SPPY*), 1, 26a (Couvreur, *Li Ki*, pp. 92–93). Cf. *Mencius*, IB, 4 (Legge, II, 156).

[260] 黎民: *Shih ching*, 258, 3 (Karlgren, p. 225), and *Shang shu*, 1, 1b, 9b (Legge, III, 17, 43): "the black-haired people."

[261] Should read in the fifteenth year (528) or, more likely, in the fourteenth year (527). For 奧 read 粤, as in *Tonggyŏng t'ongji*, 2, 30b10. *SGYS*, 3, 126, says "at the age of twenty-two" instead of twenty-six.

[262] According to *Chou li* 周禮 (*SPTK*), 5, 9a; 6, 46b–47b (Édouard Biot, *Le Tcheou-li ou Rites des Tcheou* [Peking, 1930], II, 116–118), *nei-shih* drafted documents concerning the eight functions of an emperor. Under Sui and T'ang the *Chung-shu sheng* 中書省 was changed to *Nei-shih sheng* (*HTS*, 47, 3742b) and the title *Nei-shih ling* was used from October 19, 684 (Robert Des Rotours, *Traité des fonctionnaires et Traité de l'armée*, I [Leiden, 1947], 178, n. 3). In Koryŏ, the Naesasŏng 內史省, formerly called Naeŭisŏng 內議省 and later Chungsŏsŏng 中書省, was in charge of drafting edicts and decrees (*KRS*, 76, 6b). For 舍人 see *HTS*, 47, 3742b–c (Des Rotours, I, 180–187). There were six such secretaries, all above the senior fifth rank. In Koryŏ, T'aejo established the *Naeŭi sain* 內議舍人, which was changed to *Naesa sain* 內史舍人 by King Sŏngjong in 930 and finally to *Munha sain* 門下舍人 by King Kongmin in 1369.

[263] Also called Ch'ŏdo 處道 or Yŏngch'ok. Son of King Kalmun. His name is something of a problem. *SGYS*, 3, 126, proposes that it means "hedgehog" (*YSGYS*, p. 306, n. 3); Yang, p. 201, reads it *itto* or *ich'idol* ("pessimist" or "hermit"). Yi Ki-mun reconstructs it to read **ič'ton* in *Tonga munhwa* 東亞文化, 1 (1963), 84 (*Honam munhwa yŏn'gu* 湖南文化研究, 2 [September 1964], 66, offers the same reading). In 817 Chief of Clerics Hyeryung 惠隆 and others repaired his tomb and erected a stele in his honor. Kim Pu-sik says (*SGSG*, 4, 3–4) that he has based his account on Kim Taemun's *Kyerim chapchŏn* 雞林雜傳 and *Ado hwasang pi* 阿度和尚碑 (*CKS*, I, 25), while Iryŏn (*SGYS*, 3, 126) cites as his authority *Ch'okhyangbul yebul kyŏlsamun* 髑香佛禮佛結社文 (817) by the monk Illyŏm 一念.

and deep, he advanced resolutely for the righteous cause.[264] Out of willingness to help the king fulfill his noble vow, he secretly memorialized the throne: "If Your Majesty desires to establish Buddhism, may I ask Your Majesty to pass a false decree to this officer that the king desires to initiate Buddhist activities? Once the ministers learn of this, they will undoubtedly remonstrate. Your Majesty, declaring that no such decree has been given, will then ask who has forged the royal order. They will ask Your Majesty to punish my crime, and if their request is granted,[265] they will submit to Your Majesty's will."

The king said, "Since they are bigoted and haughty, We fear they will not be satisfied even with your execution." [Yŏmch'ok] replied, "Even the deities venerate the religion of the Great Sage. If an officer as unworthy as myself is killed for its cause, miracles must happen between Heaven and Earth. If so, who then will dare to remain bigoted and haughty?" The king answered, "Our basic wish is to further the advantageous and remove the disadvantageous. But now we have to injure a loyal subject. Is this not sorrowful?" [1019a] [Yŏmch'ok] replied, "Sacrificing his life in order to accomplish goodness is the great principle of the official. Moreover, if it means the eternal brightness of the Buddha-sun and the perpetual solidarity of the kingdom, the day of my death will be the year of my birth." The king, greatly moved, praised Yŏmch'ok and said, "Though you are a commoner, your mind harbors thoughts worthy of brocaded and embroidered robes." Thereupon the king and Yŏmch'ok vowed to be true to each other.

Afterwards, a royal decree was issued, ordering the erection of a monastery in the Forest of the Heavenly Mirror, and officials in charge began construction. The court officials,[266] as expected, denounced it and expostulated with the king.[267] The king remarked, "We did not issue such an order." Thereupon Yŏmch'ok spoke out, "Indeed, I did this purposely, for if we practice Buddhism the whole country will become prosperous and peaceful. As long as it is good for the administration of the realm, what wrong can there be in forging a de-

---

264 匪直也人，秉心塞淵; *Shih ching*, 50, 3 (Karlgren, p. 33).

265 For 秦 read 奏 with A14b4.

266 For 延臣 read 廷臣, as in A14b10 and *Tonggyŏng t'ongji*, 2, 31a5.

267 面折: *Shih chi*, 9, 0038b (*MH*, II, 415); 120, 0262d2–3 (Watson, *Records of the Grand Historian of China*, II, 344): " . . . denounce people to their faces."

cree?'' Thereupon, the king called a meeting and asked the opinion of the officials. All of them remarked, ''These days monks bare their heads and wear strange garments. Their discourses are wrong and in violation of the Norm.[268] If we unthinkingly follow their proposals, there may be cause for regret. We dare not obey Your Majesty's order, even if we are threatened with death.'' Yŏmch'ok spoke with indignation, saying, ''All of you are wrong, for there must be an unusual personage before there can be an unusual undertaking. I have heard that the teaching of Buddhism is profound and arcane. We must practice it. How can a sparrow know the great ambition of a swan?''[269] The king said, ''The will of the majority is firm and unalterable.[270] You are the only one who takes a different view. I cannot follow two advices at the same time.'' He then ordered the execution [of Yŏmch'ok].

[Yŏmch'ok] then made an oath to Heaven: ''I am about to die for the sake of the Law. I pray that righteousness and the benefit [of the religion] will spread. If the Buddha has a Numen,[271] a miracle should occur after my death.'' When he was decapitated, his head flew to Diamond Mountain 金剛山,[272] falling on its summit, and white milk *(kṣīra)* gushed forth from the cut, soaring up several hundred feet.[273] The sun darkened, wonderful flowers rained from Heaven, and the earth trembled violently. The king, his officials, and the commoners, on the one hand terrified by these strange phenomena, and

---

268 非常 from *Tao te ching*, 1 (J. J. L. Duyvendak, *Tao Te Ching: The Book of the Way and Its Virtue* [Londo.., 1954], p. 17, and Arthur Waley, *The Way and Its Power* ([London, 1956], pp. 141–142), is used here ironically. Kakhun seems to imply that Buddhism, unlike Confucianism and Taoism, is indeed extraordinary, that it far surpasses in depth and breadth the tenets of the two Chinese teachings.

269 燕雀焉知鴻鵠之志哉; *Shih chi*, 48, 0164a (Watson, I, 49).

270 For 牢 in 牢不可破 as ''firm'' or ''hard'' see *Kuang ya su-cheng* 廣雅疏證 *(WYWK)*, 1B, 137–139.

271 If the Buddha is omnipotent, or if he is truly there.

272 Seven *ri* north of Kyŏngju; under Silla it was known as Northern Mountain *(TYS*, 21, 7a). According to *SGYS*, 3, 128, this took place on the fifth day of the eighth month. *SGYS*, 3, 127, says that his wife built an *araṇyaka* for the repose of his soul, which was named Chach'u hermitage 刺楸寺.

273 Compare the similar story told of Kṣāntipāla (or Ksāntivādin) 羼提波梨, who was humiliated by King Kāli (or Kaliṅga; *MBD*, I, 482a) 架(迦)梨, for which see *Damamūka sūtra* 賢愚經 2, *T*. 4, 359d-360b, esp. 360a; Édouard Chavannes, *Cinq cents contes et apologues extraits du Tripiṭaka chinois* (Paris, 1910–1934), I, 164; Thomas Watters, *On Yuan Chwang's Travels in India 629–645* A.D. (London, 1904–1905), I, 227–228. Cf. *Mahāsannipāta sūtra* 大方等大集經 (*T*. 13, 330b) and *Mahāprajñāpāramitā sūtra* (*T*. 25, 166c; Lamotte, II, 889–890), and *Seng-ch'ieh-lo-ch'a so-chi ching* 僧伽羅利所集經 (*T*. 4, 119a ff.).

on the other sorrowful for the death of the Grand Secretary, who had sacrificed his life for the cause of the Law, cried aloud and mourned. They buried his body on Diamond Mountain with due ceremony. At that time the king and his officials took an oath: "Hereafter we will worship the Buddha and revere the clergy. If we break the oath, may Heaven strike us dead."

The gentleman says:[274] "The great sage responds to the blessing of a myriad years. Goodness is born from lucky signs, and righteousness is stirred by auspices. He never fails to respond to Heaven and Earth, to be coterminous with the sun and moon, and to move the spirits, to say nothing of men.[275] For once he is confident in the Way, he will never fail to obtain assistance from Heaven and Earth. But a work is valued for its success, and a karma for its far-reaching merit. One could take up T'ai Mountain [as if it were] lighter than a feather[276] if one could make oneself truly worthy of the confidence of others. How glorious! Yŏmch'ok's death is really the proper way of dying." The same year[277] a decree forbade the taking of life. (The above is based on the national history and various documents which the author has rearranged.)

In the twenty-first year (534) trees in the Forest of the Heavenly Mirror were felled in order to build a monastery. When the ground was cleared, pillar bases, stone niches, and steps were discovered, proving the site to be that of an old monastery (*cāturdiśa*). Materials for beams and pillars came from the forest. The monastery being completed, the king abdicated and became a monk. He changed his name to Pŏpkong, mindful of the Three

---

274 Here Kakhun, like his predecessors writing in defense of the religion, borrows the lips of a gentleman to express his own views.

275 Should be punctuated as in *CPT*, I, 49. 鬼神 is translated here as "spirits," for which a number of studies exist: Ch'ien Mu, "Chung-kuo ssu-hsiang-shih chung-chih kuei-shen-kuan," *Hsin-ya hsüeh-pao*, 1 (1955), 1–43; Izushi Yoshihiko 出石誠彦, *Shina shinwa densetsu no kenkyū* 支那神話傳說の研究 (Tokyo, 1943), pp. 393–444; Nagasawa Yōji 永澤要二, *Fukushima daigaku gakugei-gakubu ronshū* 福島大學學藝學部論集, 1 (1950), 71–94; Ikeda Suetoshi 池田末利, *Hiroshima daigaku bungakubu kiyō* 廣島大學文學部紀要, 10 (1956), 206–248; Ōtani Kunihiko 大谷邦彥, *Kambungaku kenkyū* 漢文學研究, 11 (1963), 1–11, and *Chūgoku koten kenkyū* 中國古典研究, 12 (1964), 83–96. See also Wing-tsit Chan, *A Source Book in Chinese Philosophy*, pp. 789–790.

276 泰山鴻毛: from Ssu-ma Ch'ien's letter in reply to Jen Shao-ch'ing (Jen An) in *Ch'ien Han shu*, 62, 0513b19–20 (Burton Watson, *Ssu-ma Ch'ien: Grand Historian of China* [New York, 1958], p. 63): "A man has only one death. That death may be as weighty as Mount T'ai, or it may be as slight as a goose feather. It all depends upon the way he uses it."

277 Should read "the following year (529)," as in *SGSG*, 4. 4.

Garments *(trīni-cīvarāni)* and the begging bowl.[278] He aspired to lofty conduct and had compassion for all.[279] Accordingly, the monastery was named [1019b] Taewang Hŭngnyun 大王興輪 because it was the king's abode. This was the first monastery erected in Silla.[280]

The queen,[281] too, served Buddha by becoming a nun and residing at the Yŏnghŭng monastery. Since the king had patronized a great cause, he was given the posthumous epithet of Pŏphŭng 法興, which is by no means idle flattery. Thereafter, at every anniversary of Yŏmch'ok's death, an assembly was held at the Hŭngnyun monastery to commemorate his martyrdom. In the reign of King T'aejong Muyŏl 太宗武烈王 (654–661),[282] Prime Minister Kim Yang-do 金良圖,[283] whose faith was inclined westward,[284] offered his two daughters, Hwabo 花寶 and Yŏnbo 蓮寶, as maids in the monastery. The relatives of Mo Ch'ŏk 毛尺,[285] a traitor, were also reduced in rank and made to become servants. Descendants of these two kinds of people[286] serve there even today.

When I was traveling in the Eastern Capital,[287] I ascended the Diamond Mountain. Upon seeing a lonely mound and low tombstone,[288] I was unable to stop lamenting. That day, monks assembled to eat and, when asked, they

---

278   三衣瓦鉢: three kinds of robes (patch robe of nine pieces; stole of seven pieces; and inner garment of five pieces) and a begging bowl, which stand for the way of life of the Buddhist monk. See *Mahāsāṅghika* 摩訶僧祇律 23, *T*. 22, 413a27–b1, and *Ssu-fen lü hsing-shih-ch'ao* 四分律行事鈔, *T*. 40, 105a15–16.

279   For 慧悲 read 慈悲 with A16a1 and *Tonggyŏng t'ongji*, 2, 31b7.

280   We recall that the Hŭngnyun was completed only in 544 (*SGSG*, 4, 4).

281   Her religious name was Myobŏp 妙法 (*SGYS*, 3, 128–129), Pŏmnyu 法流 (*SGYS*, 1, 17), or Pŏbun 法雲 (*SGYS*, 3, 128). She died at the Yŏnghŭng monastery. For this confusion see Kim Tong-hwa (2), 9–10.

282   For 大王宗 read 太宗王 or 太宗武烈王, twenty-ninth ruler of Silla (*SGSG*, 5, 7–12; *SGYS*, 2, 61–69).

283   *SGSG*, 44, 5, has a very brief notice of Kim, who went to T'ang six times and died at the Western Capital (cf. *SGYS*, 3, 128; 5, 211–212).

284   信向西方: *SGYS*, 3, 128, reads 信向佛法. He is more inclined to Maitreya than Amitābha in *SGYS*, 5, 211–212.

285   He was executed September 11, 660, on a charge of treason (*SGSG*, 5, 10). He had escaped to Paekche and, together with Amil (*SGSG*, 47, 8), surrendered the walled town of Taeyasŏng 大耶城 (modern Hapch'ŏn) to Paekche, Silla's enemy.

286   In the original: "two kinds of copper and tin."

287   東京 or 東都: King Sŏngjong of Koryŏ established the Eastern Capital at Kyŏngju in 987 (*KRSCY*, 2, 36b-37a).

288   Cf. *SGYS*, 3, 128; Suematsu, *Shiragi-shi no shomondai*, p. 233, conjectures this tombstone to be the 栢栗寺石幢 (818).

told me it was an anniversary of the Grand Secretary's death. Indeed, the more time passed, the more dear he was thought to be. According to the inscription on Ado's tombstone, King Pŏphŭng's Buddhist name was Pŏbun 法雲, and his polite name, Pŏpkong. I have distinguished two biographies here, based on the national history and *Sui chŏn*. Those who are interested in antiquity will do well to study the matter.

The eulogy says: Usually the sovereign, with the subject's help, can keep established law but cannot innovate. Moreover, there are such factors as the appropriateness of the time and the faith of the people. Therefore, although King Wŏnjong wished to propagate Buddhism, he could not expect his order to be carried out overnight. But, thanks to the power of his original vow, the prestige of his position, and the counsel of a wise official, he succeeded in making the kingdom prosper by acts of grace[289] and became the equal of [Emperor] Ming of the Han. How great he is!—for who can carp at him? It is, however, wrong to compare him with [Emperor] Wu (464–502–549) of Liang,[290] for, while the latter served in the T'ung-t'ai monastery 同泰寺[291] as a servant and let his imperial work fall to the ground, the former [Pŏpkong] first surrendered his throne in order to install his heir and only afterwards became a monk. Of what selfishness can one accuse him? As Yŏmch'ok's career[292] attests, king and bhikṣu, though physically different, are of the same substance. Indeed, Yŏmch'ok's power was such that he could dispel the clouds of illusion, cause the wisdom-sun of Emptiness to radiate everywhere, and fly with the Buddha-sun under his arm.

289 美利利天下: *Chou i*, 1, 4b (Wilhelm, II, 1).

290 For his biography see *Liang shu*, 1, 1764d–3, 1774b; *Nan shih*, 6, 2561b–7, 2566d; *BD*, 720; Mori Mikisaburō 森三樹三郎, *Ryō no Butei* (Kyoto, 1956). He gave himself up (*she-shen* 捨身 [*adhyātma-tyāga*]) to the T'ung-t'ai monastery to serve as a menial in 527 (*Liang shu*, 3, 1771c; *Nan shih*, 7, 2564d), 529 (*Liang shu*, 3, 1771d; *Nan shih*, 7, 2564d-5a), 546 (*Nan shih*, 7, 2565d), and 547 (*Liang shu*, 3, 1773c; *Nan shih*, 7, 2565d; Mori, pp. 144–146). For his *she-shen* and Buddhist policy see Ōchō Enichi 横超慧日, *Chūgoku bukkyō no kenkyū* (Kyoto, 1958), pp. 347–352, and Ōta Teizō 太田悌藏, "Ryō Butei no shadō hōfutsu ni tsuite utagau," in *Yūki kyōju shōju kinen bukkyō shisōshi ronshū* 結城教授頌壽記念佛教思想史論集 (Tokyo, 1964), pp. 417–432.

291 For 大同寺 read 同泰寺 (completed in 527).

292 經 in 髑經 is rendered as "career" here. If, however, we omit the first logograph, as in A16b8 and *CPT*, I, 52, it should read, "The sūtra says . . ."

Pŏbun

Sŏk Pŏbun's 釋法雲 secular name was Kongnŭngjong 公麦宗, his posthumous epithet Chinhŭng 眞興 (534–540–576).[293] He was the brother of King Pŏphŭng and the son of King Kalmun 葛文王 (500–514).[294] His mother's maiden name was Kim. He ascended the throne at the age of seven years. Rightly indulgent and rightly benevolent,[295] he attended strictly to business and punctually observed his promises.[296] He rejoiced at hearing the good and strove to uproot the evil.

In the seventh year (544)[297] of his reign the Hŭngnyun monastery was completed, and the common people were permitted to enter the clergy. In the eighth year (545) he ordered the *Tae ach'an* 大阿湌 Kŏch'ilpu 居柒夫[298] and others to gather learned men to compile a national history. In the tenth year (549) [the state of] Liang dispatched an envoy, together with the

---

293 Twenty-fourth king of Silla. In 553 he recaptured from Paekche fortifications on the lower reaches of the Han and in 562 subjugated the state of Kaya (Karak), thus extending Silla sway to the Naktong River basin. In order to prepare for border invasions, he established provinces and installed battalions along the Han; in order to expand his territory and to exalt national prestige, he made a tour of the country and had stone monuments erected at the sites of inspection. See *SGSG*, 4, 4–7; *SGYS*, 2, 55–56; 3, 128–129. For his *Sunsu pi* 巡狩碑 see *CKS*, I, 6–12; *SG*, 2 (1930), 69–90; and *Sach'ong* 史叢, 1 (1955), 66–77.

294 An honorary or posthumous title given to the father (e.g., *SGSG*, 2, 5), father-in-law (e.g., *SGSG*, 1, 8), grandfather-in-law (e.g., *SGSG*, 2, 5), or maternal uncle of a king (e.g., *SGSG*, 4, 8), as well as to the consort of a queen (e.g., *SGYS*, 1, 20). For Suematsu's summary of previous studies, except for Kim Sang-gi's in *CH*, 5 (1936), 181–201, and his own view see *Shiragi-shi no sho-mondai*, pp. 186–205. For the reconstruction of the word *kalmun*, meaning "deceased" or "hidden," see *SGYS*, 1, 46 (Yang, pp. 165–167).

295 克寬克仁: *Shang shu*, 4, 3b (Legge, III, 180).

296 敬事而信: *Analects*, I, 5 (Waley, p. 84).

297 Should be the second month (March 10–April 7) of the fifth year (544), as in *SGSG*, 4, 4.

298 Should be the seventh month (July 25–August 22) of the sixth year (545). *Tae ach'an* is the name of the fifth rank, granted only to those above the *chin'gol* 眞骨. The color of their official robe was purple (*SGSG*, 33, 1; 38, 1). Kŏch'ilpu's surname was Kim; he was a fifth-generation descendant of King Naemul. He is said to have visited Koguryŏ and transmitted some Buddhist scriptures to Hyeryang. In 551, together with seven other generals, he seized the area north of Chungnyŏng 竹嶺 from Koguryŏ, and in 576 he was honored with the highest title, *Sangdaedŭng* 上大等 (or *Sangsin* 上臣; initiated in 531; *SGSG*, 38, 2). He died at the age of seventy-eight (*SGSG*, 44, 2–3; *TYS*, 21, 35a–b).

student monk Kaktŏk 覺德 [who had studied abroad], and some relics.[299] The king sent officials to welcome them in front of the Hŭngnyun monastery. In the fourteenth year (553) he ordered construction of a new palace, east of Wŏlsŏng 月城,[300] and a yellow dragon [1019c] was seen on the spot. The king, moved by the sight, changed it into a monastery and named it the Hwangnyong ("Yellow Dragon") monastery 黃龍寺.[301] In the twenty-sixth year (565) the Ch'en (557–589) sent an envoy, Liu Ssu 劉思, and the monk Myŏnggwan 明觀 with more than 700 rolls of scriptures and treatises. In the twenty-seventh year (566) the two monasteries Chiwŏn 祇園 and Silche 實際[302] were completed, as was the Hwangnyong monastery too. In the tenth month of the thirty-third year (572) the king held a *P'algwanhoe* 八關會 ("Assembly of the Eight Commandments")[303] for the repose of

---

299 See *SGSG*, 4, 5. *Liang shu*, 54, 1841d (section on Silla) and 3, 1773d (under *t'ai-ch'ing* 3) is silent about the event.

300 Five *ri* southeast of Kyŏngju. In 101 King P'asa ordered the construction of a palace in the shape of a half-moon, hence the name. Yi Il-lo wrote a seven-word *ku-shih* about the place, which is preserved in the *Tongmun sŏn* 東文選 (1914), 6, 87–88. For the remains excavated in 1915 see *CG*, 14 (1959), 489–502. See also *TYS*, 21, 22b–23a.

301 Also written 皇龍 (*SGSG*, 4, 6 and 7 and *SGYS*, 3, 132) or 皇隆 (*SGYS* 4, 180, 184; *HKSC*, 13, 524a). The site of the monastery is in Kyŏngju, Naedong myŏn 內東面, Kuhwang ri 九黃里. It had, in its precincts, two of the three national treasures of Silla, an image of Buddha and a nine-story pagoda. It was burned down in 1238 during the Mongol invasion (*KRS*, 23, 33b; *TYS*, 21, 30a–b). See n. 236 above.

302 "In the second month of spring," according to *SGSG*, 4, 6. Chiwŏn is Jetavana, the name of the grove at Śrāvastī where Buddha often dwelt and preached (*BHSD*, p. 244a); Silche renders the Sanskrit *bhūtakoṭi* (*BHSD*, p. 410b). Cf. *SGYS*, 5, 236.

303 *SGSG*, 4, 7, specifies "on the twentieth day of the tenth month (November 10)." The first meeting in Koryŏ was held in 918 (*KRS*, 1, 14b; 69, 32b–33a). In the eleventh month of 981, however, the ceremony was simplified when King Sŏngjong (960–982–997) ordered that the "unorthodox and disturbing" games and shows accompanying the ceremony be prohibited (*KRS*, 3, 1b); in 987 the king ordered that the ceremony, hitherto held in Kaesŏng and the Western Capital, be discontinued (*KRS*, 3, 13a; 69, 33a). In 993, when the Khitans invaded, Yi Chi-baek 李知白 requested the resumption of the ceremony, emphasizing its efficacy in the war against the northern hordes (*KRS*, 94, 3a–b). At last, in 1010, after an interval of twenty-four years, the observance was revived on Ch'oe Hang's 崔沆 (972–1061) proposal (*KRS*, 4, 6a; 69, 33a), only to be discontinued until 1034 (*KRS*, 6, 1b). For a period of about 130 years, from the time of King Chŏngjong 靖宗 (1018–1035–1046) to the reign of Ŭijong 毅宗 (1127–1147–1170–1173), the *p'algwanhoe* was held regularly. In 1179, however, the expenses for the ceremony became an issue again and it was suspended. It was revived in 1225, especially after the transfer of the capital to Kanghwa Island 江華島 (1232) during the Mongol invasion. It was held frequently there, perhaps to pray for the retreat of the enemy from Korean shores (*KRS*, 23, 27b–28a). The fervor for the ceremony began to decline in the thirteenth century, owing partly to the frequent coastal raids of Japanese pirates. The last *p'algwanhoe* of Koryŏ took place in the eleventh month of 1391 (*KRS*, 46, 28b). Normally the ceremony took place on the fourteenth and

officers and soldiers killed in action. The ceremony was held in the outer monastery and lasted for seven days. In the thirty-fifth year (574) a Buddha image sixteen feet high[304] was cast at the Hwangnyong monastery. Tradition says that it was cast with the gold which King Aśoka shipped to Sap'o 絲浦.[305] The story is recorded in the biography of Chajang. In the thirty-sixth year (575) tears from the image flowed down to its heels.[306] In the thirty-seventh year (576) the *wŏnhwa* 原花[307] was first chosen as *sŏllang* 仙郎.

At first the king and his officials were perplexed by the problem of finding a way to discover the talented. They wished to have people disport themselves in groups so that they could observe their behavior and thus elevate [the talented among] them to positions of service. Therefore two beautiful girls, Nammu 南無[308] and Chunjŏng 俊貞,[309] were selected, and a group of about three hundred people gathered around them. But the two girls competed with each other, and Chunjŏng, after making friendly overtures to Nammu and plying her with wine till she was drunk, drowned her in the river. The group became discordant and abandoned the activity. Afterwards, handsome youths were chosen instead. They powdered their faces,[310] wore ornamented dresses,

---

fifteenth days of the eleventh month. From 1041 to 1120, however, the ceremonies were also held in the tenth month, perhaps as subsidiary ones. For the ceremony in T'ang China see *SZ*, 46 (1935), 1226–1227. For the Korean ceremony see *Tongguk sahak* 東國史學, 4 (1956), 31–54; *CG*, 9 (1956), 235–251; and *Yesul nonmunjip* 藝術論文集, 1 (1962), 92–108.

304 The normal height of the Buddha in his worldly transformation (*nirmāṇakāya*) appearing for the benefit of living beings.

305 Originally called Kurahwa 屈阿火. King P'asa made it a *hyŏn* 縣; King Kyŏngdok changed its name to Hagok 河曲 (or Hasŏ 河西); later, Koryŏ T'aejo changed its name to Ulchu 蔚州 (*SGYS*, 3, 136; *TYS*, 22, 1a–2a). For the gold Aśoka was supposed to have shipped see *SGYS*, 3, 136–137. The image was cast either in the third month (April 7-May 6; *SGSG*, 4, 7) or on the seventeenth day of the tenth month (November 16 according to *Sajung ki* 寺中記, quoted in *SGYS*, 3, 136). The total weight of the image was 35,007 斤, and it required 10,198 分 of gold. The story is found not in the biography of Chajang, as *HKC* says, but in *SGYS*, 3, 136–137.

306 Similar stories are recorded in *SGSG*. In the tenth month of 400, King Naemul's beloved horse shed tears, presaging the death of the king in the second month of 402 (3, 3). In 646 a statue of King Tongmyŏng's mother shed tears of blood for three days, lamenting the great loss of lives during the war against T'ang in 644 (21, 9).

307 Or 源花. Female leaders of the *hwarang* institution before they were replaced by handsome boys. Yi Pyŏng-do, in *Han'guk sa*, I, 599, proposes that this change took place in the early part of Chinhŭng's reign (540–576) rather than in 576, as *SGSG*, 4, 7, has it.

308 *SGSG*, 4, 7, reads 南毛.

309 *SGYS*, 3, 153, has Kyojŏng 姣貞.

310 For 傳粉 read 傳粉, which is Kakhun's insertion, originally not in *SGSG*, 4, 7. For 粉飾 see *Han-shih wai-chuan* 韓詩外傳 (*SPTK*), 5, 16b (James R. Hightower, *Han Shih Wai Chuan*

and were respected as *hwarang* 花郞,[311] and men of various sorts gathered around them. They instructed one another in the Way and in righteousness, entertained each other with songs and music, or went sightseeing to famous mountains and rivers, no matter how far away. From all this a man's moral character can be discerned, and the good were recommended to the court.

Kim Tae-mun 金大問,[312] in his [*Hwarang*] *segi* 花郞世記 (Annals of the hwarang), remarks: "Henceforth, able ministers and loyal subjects are chosen from them, and good generals and brave soldiers are born therefrom." Ch'oe Ch'i-wŏn 崔致遠 (857--?)[313] in his preface to the *Nallang pi* 鸞郞碑序 (Inscription on the tomb of Knight Nan) says: "There is a wonderful and mysterious way in the country, called *p'ungnyu* 風流,[314] which in fact em-

---

[Cambridge, 1952], p. 187) (cf. *Shih chi*, 126, 0271d). *T.* 14, 434c2–3, reads that the facial coloring of people in a country about to be blessed by a visit of Maitreya has the tint of peach blossoms. Kim Yŏng-t'ae 金煐泰, in *Pulgyo hakpo*, 3–4 (1966), 147, writes that the *hwarang* practice of powdering their faces might have been suggested by this passage.

311 For a consideration of and a bibliography on the *hwarang*, which Yang reads as *pallae* (pp. 184–188, 242–243; *SGYS*, 3, 153), see my *Studies in the Saenaennorae*, pp. 139–140, n. 133.

312 He studied in T'ang and in 704 became the *Hansanju todok* 漢山州都督. All his works are known only by titles (*SGSG*, 44, 3–5; *TYS*, 21, 36b).

313 Perhaps the most celebrated Korean writer of all time. In 868 he left for T'ang, where after six years of study he became a *chin-shih* and held the post of the *Chiang-nan-tao Hsüan-chou p'iao-shui-hsien-wei* 江南道宣州漂水縣尉 and other offices. When the Huang Ch'ao 黃巢 rebellion broke out (874), Ch'oe served under Kao Pien 高駢 (d. 887), the *Huai-nan-tao chieh-tu-shih* 淮南道節度使, as his secretary and drafted memorials, manifestos, and other missives. When Hui-tsung (862–873–888) learned of Ch'oe's intention to return to Silla, he conferred upon him the rank of ambassador and commissioned him as an envoy to the peninsula (885). King Hyŏnjong 顯宗 (992–1010–1031) of Koryŏ granted him the posthumous title and enfeoffed him as Marquis of Munch'ang 文昌侯 (1023). His tablet was placed in the Confucian Temple in 1020 (*KRS*, 4, 34a) or in 1116 (*KRS*, 62, 42b). His writings include the *Kyewŏn p'ilgyŏng chip* 桂苑筆耕集 (*SPTK*) and *Fa-tsang ho-shang chuan* 法藏和尙傳 (*T.* 50, no. 2054). For his poems contained in the *Tongmun sŏn* see 4, 49–50; 9, 156; 12, 218–219; 19, 346, 355–356. Ch'oe appears in the *I-wen chih* of *HTS*, 60, 3773b. See *SGSG*, 46, 2–4; *CMP*, 247, 1a; 246, 25b; *TYS*, 21, 36a–b.

314 設敎之源 備詳仙史 in *SGSG*, 4, 7, which comes after 風流, is omitted in our text. *P'ungnyu* (*feng-liu*) is a prize specimen in the cabinet of untranslatable critical terms which enjoyed a vogue in medieval China. According to Ogawa Tamaki, who has studied the shifts in its meaning, the term appears generally in the preface or critical estimate of the *Hou Han shu* (e.g., chapters 83, 86, 91, 112A, 113) in the classical sense of "moral influence," "customs and manners," or "vestiges of customs." From the Three Kingdoms period, it began to lose its political and moralistic connotations and became related to individual character. Under the Chin, it definitely became a fashionable term for that which demanded one's respect or attracted the attention of one's contemporaries. Shorn of its original meaning, the term ultimately became associated with the famous gentlemen (*ming-shih*), emphasis falling this time on "freedom of spirit," "revolt against convention," or "free play of emotion,"; hence it denoted an aesthetically praiseworthy, rather than a morally praiseworthy, quality. See

braces the Three Teachings and transforms myriad men. It is a tenet of the
Minister of Crime of Lu 魯司寇[315] that one should be filial to one's parents
and loyal to one's sovereign; it is the belief of the Keeper of Archives of Chou
周柱史[316] that one should be at home in the action of inaction and practice the
wordless doctrine; and it is the teaching of the Indian prince that one should
avoid evil and do many good deeds." Also, Ling-hu Ch'eng 令狐澄[317] of
T'ang, in the *Hsin-lo kuo-chi* (Record of Silla) 新羅國記,[318] states that "the
hwarang were chosen from the handsome sons of the nobles and their faces
were made up. They were called *hwarang*, and were respected and served by
their countrymen.[319] This was a way to facilitate the king's government."
According to the [*Hwarang*] *segi*, from *wŏnhwa* to the end of Silla there were
more than 200 knights, of whom the "Four Knights"[320] were the wisest.

The king ascended the throne as a child and worshiped Buddha ardently.
In his late years he shaved his head and became a monk. After he had donned
a Buddhist robe he styled himself Pŏbun ("Clouds of the Law"). He received

Kokugo kokubun, 20 (1951), 514–526. For its usage in the *Shih-shuo hsin-yü* 世說新語, Professor
Richard B. Mather writes that the term was used six times, always in the sense of "cultivated manners," "urbanity," "refinement," or "aesthetic sensitivity." The quality was greatly admired by
aristocratic famous gentlemen and even by the cultivated Buddhist monks who kept company with
the gentlemen. For further studies on the term see Hoshikawa Kiyotaka 星川清孝, "Shindai ni okeru
fūryū no rinen no seiritsu katei ni tsuite," *Ibaragi daigaku bunrigakubu kiyō* 茨城大學文理學部紀要,
1 (1951), 93–104; 2 (1952), 100–114, and "Fūryū no shisō to Chūgoku bungaku," *Shibun*, 9 (1954),
11–25.

315 Confucius is said to have held this office (e.g., *Shih chi*, 47, 0161b; *MH*, V, 319, n. 3), for which
see H. G. Creel, *Confucius, the Man and the Myth* (New York, 1945), pp. 37–38; p. 300, n. 17. For
the functions of Ssu-k'ou see *Shang shu*, 2, 2b (Legge, III, 529–530).

316 *Shih chi*, 63, 0180c-d.

317 In his *Ta-chung i-shih* 大中遺事, Ling-hu quotes *Hsin-lo kuo-chih*, in *Shuo fu* 說郛, 49, 1b.

318 By Ku Yin 顧愔 (*HTS*, 220, 4149d), who as secretary accompanied the T'ang envoy Kuei
Ch'ung-ching 歸崇敬, who held the office of *Ts'ang-pu lang-chung* 倉部郎中 (Des Rotours, I, 79).
According to *SGSG*, 9, 6, T'ang T'ai-tsung sent Kuei to invest the Silla king and the king's mother
(768).

319 End of quotation from *SGSG*, 4, 7.

320 Namsŏkhaeng 南石行 (or Namnang 南郎), Sullang 述郎, Yŏngnang 永郎, and An Sang 安詳.
Among the scenic spots they visited, the most famous was Samilp'o 三日浦, celebrated in many
Korean poems. Tradition has it that once four knights came here to admire the beauty of the Diamond
Mountains and did not return for three days, hence the name. There was a small peak to the south,
on top of which was a stone niche, and on the north precipice of this peak were six Chinese logographs
in red ink which read "We are going toward the South." See my *Anthology of Korean Poetry* (New
York, 1964). p. 95; *TYS*, 45, 13a-14b; *Chibong yusŏl* 芝峯類說 (*CKK*, 1909), 18, 245; *P'aegwan
chapki* 稗官雜記 (*CKK*, 1904), 4, 580–581.

and retained the commandments and purified the three kinds of acts *(trini-karmāni)*[321] until his death. Upon his death the people buried him with ceremony on the peak north of the Aegong monastery 哀公寺.[322] In that year the master of the Law Anham 安含 arrived from Sui, the account of which will be related in his biography.

[1020a] The eulogy says: Great is the power of custom over man. Therefore, if the king wants to change the fashion of an age, no one can prevent his success, which follows like the downflow of water. After [King] Chinhŭng first worshiped Buddhism and initiated the way of the *hwarang*, people gladly followed him and imitated his example.[323] Their excitement was as great as when visiting a treasure house or when going to the spring terrace.[324] The [king's] aim was to make the people progress toward goodness[325] and justice and to lead them to the Great Way.[326] Emperor Ai 哀帝 (26–7–1B.C.)[327] of the [Former] Han loved only lust. Pan Ku 班固 (32–92)[328] therefore remarked, "The tenderness[329] which seduces man belongs not only to woman, but to man as well." This indeed cannot be compared with our story [of the *hwarang*].

---

321 Purity of action, speech, and deed; see *Saṁyuktāgama* 別譯雜阿含經 5, *T.* 2, 403c19–22; [*Abhidharma*] *jñānaprasthāna* 阿毘達磨發智論 11, *T.* 26, 972b9–10; and *Mahāvibhāṣā* 大毘婆沙論 113, *T.* 27, 587b, 1–12.

322 Both Kings Pŏphŭng and Chinhŭng were buried on the hill north of this monastery (*SGYS*, 1, 17b; *SGSG*, 4, 4 and 7). According to *SGYS*, there are also tombstones of King Chinji (1, 19b) and King T'aejong (2, 62). Eda Shunyū thinks that this monastery may not have existed then because the first monastery was only completed in 544 (*Bunka*, 2 [1935], 982).

323 For 倣効 read 倣劾. *CPT*, I, 55, reads 劾倣.

324 春臺: *Tao te ching*, 30 (Duyvendak, p. 55; Waley, p. 168).

325 遷善: *Mencius*, VIIA, 13 (Legge, II, 455).

326 鴻漸: *Chou i*, 5, 13b–14a (Wilhelm, I, 219).

327 *Ch'ien Han shu*, 11, 0315d–0316c (Dubs, III, 15–39).

328 For his biography see *Hou Han shu*, 70A, 0784a–70b, 0788c, and *BD*, 1600.

329 For 柔曼 see *Shih chi*, 125, 0270a–c (Watson, II, 462 ff.), and *Ch'ien Han shu*, 93, 0595a.

Kaktŏk

Sŏk Kaktŏk 釋覺德 was a native of Silla. He was sagacious and erudite, and his holiness was unfathomable. Since Buddhism had been practiced in Silla, people strove to embrace the faith. The master knew how to transform the world with his all-embracing wisdom. It is said that [a bird] must leave the [dark] valley to mount the high tree[330] and that [a man] must seek a teacher in order to study the Way. If one lives at ease and acts slowly, one betrays the original purpose of Śākyamuni's renunciation.[331] He, therefore, went to Liang by sea and became a pioneer in the search for the Law; but we do not know in what year this was. This, then, was the beginning of study abroad for Silla nationals.

He studied under brilliant teachers and from their mouths received instructions[332] which were so enlightening that he felt as if the white film on his eyes had been lifted and a tumor removed.[333] He studied without idleness and omission.[334] His virtuous deeds were lofty, and his religious fame spread more and more. [He thought] it the duty of the treasure seeker not only to help himself but also to help the poor of his own country. Therefore, in the tenth year of King Chinhŭng (549) he returned to the old capital with a Liang envoy[335] who brought relics. The king ordered officials[336] to go out and welcome them with due ceremony [1020b] in front of the Hŭngnyun monastery. This, too, was the beginning [of the worship] of relics [in Silla]. In former days Seng-hui[337] went to Wu in order to make progress and in seven days secured

---

330 遷喬: *Shih ching*, 165, 1 (Karlgren, pp. 108–109); *Mencius*, IIIA, 15 (Legge, II, 255).

331 *CPT*, I, 51, reads 報恩之本意 for 棄————.

332 A19b2 and *CPT*, I, 51, read 訣 for 訊.

333 In esoteric Buddhism one of the symbolic rites that accompany the initiation ceremony is the removal of the membrane of ignorance *(ajñāna)* by the master in the name of Buddha (*HBGR*, pp. 232b, 236a, 261a-b).

334 無荒無怠: *Shang shu*, 2, 2a (Legge, III, 55).

335 *SGSG*, 4, 5. According to *SGYS*, 3, 127, his name was Shen Hu 沈湖, who is said to have come in the beginning of the era *t'ai-ch'ing* (547–549).

336 有司: *Shang shu*, 2, 3b (Legge, III, 59).

337 When Seng-hui arrived in Nanking in 247, Sun Ch'üan of Wu asked him to perform a miracle (that is, to produce a relic). Seng-hui prayed and worshiped in front of a copper flask for a week, but nothing happened. Finally, after three weeks' prayer, a relic emanating five-colored radiance was

supernatural efficacy. At a time when the sovereign had already manifested his faith, the master, accompanied by an important envoy from Liang,[338] returned to his country. Kaktŏk [therefore] experienced no obstacles [in propagating the faith].[339] He infused the universe with the waters of the Dharma and made the lazy cherish the ambition to follow [his example].[340] The merits he achieved and benefits he conferred—what superior acts they were!

Twenty-six years later,[341] the Ch'en sent an envoy, Liu Ssu, and a Silla monk studying in China, Myŏnggwan, with more than 2,700 rolls of Buddhist scriptures and treatises.[342] At first, when Buddhism in Silla was relatively new, the collection of scriptures and images was poor. It was not until this time that everything began to take shape. We do not know how the lives of these two masters ended.

---

found in the flask. See *KSC*, 1, 325b (Chavannes [5], 203–205), and Gustav Ecke and Paul Demiéville, *The Twin Pagodas of Zayton* (Cambridge, 1935), p. 57, n. 87. See also n. 102 above.

338 上國 in the original.

339 A lacuna after 艱 is reconstructed by *CPT*, I, 52, as 礙.

340 A lacuna after 立 is reconstructed by *CPT*, I, 52, as 表.

341 Should read sixteen years later, for the Ch'en envoy is said to have come in 565. In *SGSG*, 4, 6, and *SGYS*, 3, 150, this event is correctly entered under *t'ien-chia* 6. In *SGYS*, 3, 127, the reign title is miswritten as *t'ien-shou* 天壽.

342 1,700 rolls in *SGSG*, 4, 6, and *SGYS*, 3, 150; in the biography of Pŏbun, only 700 rolls.

Chimyŏng

Sŏk Chimyŏng 釋智明 was a native of Silla. He was spiritually awakened, and he acted in an appropriate manner. He accumulated merit and adhered to the disciplines.[343] Always ready to praise others' virtues, he tried to incorporate them within himself. He was most generous with men; in truth, his deeds, great and high,[344] were worthy of notice.

In the earlier stage of the spread of Buddhism in Korea, few people were interested. But occasionally the talented came forth, raising their arms[345] to follow the cause. They either attained enlightenment through the use of their talent or went to a distant country to seek the Law. When the new physician is overwhelmed[346] by the old, then only are the right and wrong distinguished. When a former magistrate briefs a new one, he hands down instructions like a teacher. Therefore people went west to China one after another and returned after attaining a thorough comprehension [of the truth]. The master, a genius commanding the admiration of the world, sought the Law[347] in [the state of] Ch'en in the seventh month, autumn, of the seventh year of King Chinp'yŏng 眞平王 (585).[348] He traveled both by land and by sea, one moment to the east and the next to the west. If there was one who was known for his way or his fame, the master never failed to seek him out and ask his guidance, just as wood is made straight by the use of a plumb line[349] or raw gold is fashioned into a vessel. He left, and before he knew it, ten years had already passed, during which time he mastered the essence of

---

343 密行: *Miao-fa lien-hua ching* 妙法蓮華經 4, *T.* 9, 30a (Hendrik Kern, *The Saddharma-puṇḍarika or the Lotus of the True Law* [Oxford, 1884], p. 210): "Unknown in this *course of duty* to Rāhula . . . " (italics mine). W. E. Soothill does not translate this line in *The Lotus of the Wonderful Law* (Oxford, 1930), p. 148.

344 顯顯卬卬: *Shih ching*, 252, 6 (Karlgren, p. 210).

345 奮臂: *Shih chi*, 6, 0027a (*MH*, II, 235).

346 According to the *K'ang-hsi tzu-tien (WYKW)*, pp. 938 and 935, 揜 is another graphic form of 揜, meaning "overshadow," "harass," or "overwhelm." I owe this reference to Professor Fang Chao-ying of Columbia University.

347 問津利往: *Analects*, XVIII, 6 (Waley, p. 219).

348 *SGSG*, 4, 8.

349 如木從繩: *Shang shu*, 5, 9b (Legge, III, 253); *Hsün tzu*, 1, 7a (Dubs, p. 31); and *Han Fei tzu (SPPY)*, 2, 5a (Burton Watson, *Han Fei Tzu: Basic Writings* [New York, 1964], p. 28).

learning. Eager to introduce the lamp of Buddhism at home, in the ninth month of the twenty-fourth year of King Chinp'yŏng (602)[350] he went back to his country with a returning Silla envoy. The king, deeply impressed by his fame, entertained a high regard for him, respected the *śila* and *vinaya*, rewarded him with the title of *Taedŏk (Bhadanta)* 大德, and encouraged those who were so disposed to follow in his way. The master was as high as Mount Sung 嵩 or Mount Hua[351] [in his moral stature] and as deep as a wide ocean in his magnanimity. He enlightened disciples with [the brightness of] the wisdom-moon and encouraged them with [the constancy of] a virtuous wind. The clergy and laity regarded his teachings as their unchanging rule and great lesson.[352] Later the king rewarded him [with the title of] *Taedaedŏk* 大大德. Even in daily life he kept strict discipline. We do not know where he died.

The master was the first to go to Ch'en. Five years after him, the master of the Law Wŏn'gwang 圓光 went to Ch'en; eight years after, Tamyuk 曇育[353] went to Sui and returned home seven years later with Hyemun 惠文,[354] a Silla envoy to China. Both [Tamyuk] and Chimyŏng, distinguished for their virtues and wonderful gifts,[355] won fame in their time. We cannot value one above the other.

The eulogy says: Chi Cha 季札[356] studied music in the house of Chou, and Confucius asked Lao Tan about propriety.[357] They did not start a new school of thought, but based their learning on an already established authority. [Kak]tŏk and others went to study in an advanced country and returned [after] attaining the Way. Although they differed [from Chi Cha and Confucius], they shared the same aspirations.

---

350 *SGSG*, 4, 9.

351 With *CPT*, I, 57, line 12, read 華 for 蕐, which does not appear in either the *Lung-k'an shou-chien* 龍龕手鑑 or the *K'ang-hsi tzu-tien*.

252 是彝是訓: *Shang shu*, 7, 4a (Legge, III, 332). *CPT*, I, 57, reads 緇素之德 for ————徒.

353 Went to Sui in 596 (*SGSG*, 4, 9) and returned in 605 (*SGSG*, 4, 10).

354 Went to Sui in the seventh month of 604 and returned to Silla in the third month of 605 (*SGSG*, 4, 10). The above passages are something of a problem because of their confusing chronology. Actually, Chimyŏng went to Ch'en in 585, Wŏn'gwang in 589, Tamyuk to Sui in 596, and Tamyuk returned with Hyemun in 605. Hence "eight years after" and "seven years later" are misleading. I follow here and below the punctuation in *CPT*.

355 才之美: *Analects*, VIII, 11 (Legge, I, 212).

356 *Shih chi*, 31, 0121c ff. (*MH*, IV, 6 ff.).

357 仲尼問禮於老聃: *Shih chi*, 47, 0161a (*MH*, V, 299–301, esp. 299, n. 4).

Wŏn'gwang

[1020c] Sŏk Wŏn'gwang's 釋圓光 secular name was Sŏl 薛 or Pak 朴.[358] He was a resident of the capital of Silla. At the age of thirteen he shaved his head and became a monk. (The *Hsü kao-seng chuan* says he shaved his head after he went to T'ang.)[359] His Supernal Vessel[360] was free and magnificent, and his understanding beyond the ordinary. He was versed in the works of *hsüan-hsüeh* and Confucianism and loved literature. Being lofty in thought, he intensely disliked the world of passion[361] and retired at thirty to a cave on Samgi Mountain 三岐山.[362] His shadow never appeared outside the cave.

One day a bhikṣu came to a place near the cave and there built a hermitage (*āraṇya*)[363] to cultivate the way of religion. One night while the master was sitting and reciting scriptures a spirit called to him, "Excellent! There are many religious people, yet none excels you. Now this bhikṣu is cultivating black art; but because of your pure thought my way is blocked,[364] and I have not been able to approach him. Whenever I pass by him, however, I cannot help thinking badly of him. I beseech you to persuade him to move away; if he does not follow my advice,[365] there shall be a disaster." The following morning the master went to the monk and told him, "You had better move away to avoid disaster, or [if you stay] it will not be to your advantage." But [the monk] remarked, "When I undertake to do something opposed by Māra himself, why should I worry about what a demon[366] has to say?"

---

358 Bothe *HKSC*, 13, 523c, and *SGYS*, 4, 170, have Pak, while *SGYS*, 4, 181, based on the *Sui chŏn*, has Sŏl as his surname.

359 *HKSC*, 13, 523c.

360 神器: *Tao te ching*, 28 (Duyvendak, p. 79).

361 A21b5 reads 慎閙 for 情閙.

362 Thirty *ri* north of Kyŏngju, Pihwa hyŏn 比火縣 of Silla; King Kyŏngdŏk changed its name to the present one (*TYS*, 21, 4a).

363 "Dwelling in the forest" (*BHSD*, p. 102b; *HBGR*, pp. 34b–35a). According to the *Kobon sui chŏn*, quoted in *SGYS*, a bhikṣu came to the place four years after Wŏn'gwang retired to the mountain, while the incident took place two years after the bhikṣu built his hermitage.

364 In *SGYS*, this statement refers to the spirit: "His clamorous chanting of spells disturbs my peace. . . ."

365 There is a lacuna of one logograph. *SGYS*, 4, 182, reads: 若久往者 恐我忽作罪業.

366 *SGYS*, 4, 182, reads 至行者爲魔所眩 法師何愛狐鬼之言乎. "How could a cultivator of right

The same evening the spirit returned and asked for the monk's reply. The master, fearful of the spirit's anger, said that he had not yet been to the monk, but that he knew the monk would not dare disobey. The spirit, however, remarked, "I have already ascertained the truth. Be quiet and you shall see." That same night there was a sound as loud as thunder. At dawn the master went out and saw that the hermitage had been crushed under a landslide. Later the spirit returned and said, "I have lived for several thousand years and possess unequaled power to change things. This is, therefore, nothing to be marveled at." He also advised the master: "Now the master has benefited himself (*ātmahitam*), but lacks [the merit of] benefiting others (*parahitam*). Why not go to China to obtain the Law of Buddha, which will be of great benefit for future generations?" "It has been my cherished desire to learn the Way in China," replied the master, "but owing to the obstacles of sea and land I am afraid I cannot get there." Thereupon the spirit told him in detail of matters relating to a journey to the West.

In the third month, spring, of the twelfth year of King Chinp'yŏng (590),[367] the master went to Ch'en. He traveled to various lecture halls, received and noted subtle instructions. After mastering the essence of the *Tattvasiddhi* 成實,[368] the *Nirvaṇā*, and several treatises from the *Tripiṭaka*,[369] he went to Hu-ch'iu 虎丘[370] in Wu, [now] harboring an ambition which soared to the sky. Upon the request of a believer, the master expounded the *Tattvasiddhi*, and thenceforth requests from his admirers came one after another like the close succession of scales [on a fish].

At that time Sui soldiers marched into Yang-tu 楊都.[371] Here the com-

---

practice be blinded by a demon? Why should the master of the Law be afraid of what a bogey says?"

367 With *SGSG*, 4, 9, this should read "the eleventh year (589)."

368 By Harivarman (*ca.* 250–350), translated by Kumārajīva (*T.* 32, 239a–373b). I follow here Leon Hurvitz's suggestion in *JAOS*, 85 (1965), 391 and 451, and read *Tattvasiddhi*.

369 Miyamoto Shōson points out that the *shu* 數 refers to Abhidharma and the *ron* 論 to *Tattvasiddhi* (*Bukkyō kenkyū*, 2 [1938], 16–18).

370 Hu-ch'iu, northwest of Wu (Su-chou), Kiangsu, was one of the Buddhist centers in the region east of Chien-k'ang, the capital of the Eastern Chin. In 368 Wang Hsün 王珣 (350–401) (*Chin shu*, 65, 1255c-d) and his younger brother Wang Min 王珉 (351–398) (*Chin shu*, 65, 1255d) had two monasteries built on this mountain (*T.* 49, 781b1–2). Ch'u Tao-i 竺道壹 (*KSC*, 6, 357a–b), Seng-min 僧旻 (*HKSC*, 5, 461c), and Seng-ch'üan 僧詮 (*KSC*, 7, 369c) all stayed on this mountain at one time or another.

371 Capital of Ch'en, modern Nanking. Sui Wen-ti (541–581–604), together with Generals Ho-jo Pi 賀若弼 and Han Ch'in-fu 韓擒虎, attacked the city and the Hou-chu of Ch'en (Shu-pao, 553–

mander of the army saw a tower in flame. But when he went to the rescue, there was no sign of fire,[372] and he found only the master tied up in front of the tower. Greatly amazed, [the commander] set him free. It was during the era *k'ai-huang* 開皇 (590–600) that the *Mahāyānasaṃgraha* 攝論[373] was first spread, and the master cherished its style; he won great acclaim in the [Sui] capital.

Now that he had further cultivated meritorious works, it was incumbent on him to continue the spread of the Law eastward. Our country therefore appealed to Sui, and a decree allowed him to return to his country in the twenty-second year, *kyŏngsin*, of [King] Chinp'yŏng (600)[374] together with the *Naema* 奈麻 Chebu 諸父[375] and the *Taesa* 大舍[376] Hoengch'ŏn 橫川, who at that time served as envoys to China. On the sea, a strange being suddenly appeared out of the water and paid homage to the master, saying, "Would the master please erect a monastery and expound the truth there for my sake so that your disciples could gain outstanding rewards?" The master complied. Because he had returned after an absence of some years, old and young alike rejoiced, and even the king declared his pious respect and regarded him as the "Mighty in Kindness."

[1021a] One day Wŏn'gwang returned to his old retreat on Samgi Mountain. At midnight the same spirit visited the master and asked him about his experiences abroad. [The master] thanked him and said, "Thanks to your gracious protection, all my wishes have been fulfilled." "I will not desert

---

582–589–604) was captured. See Otto Franke, *Geschichte des chinesischen Reiches* (Berlin and Leipzig, 1930–1952), II, 181–182, III, 283 (*Tzu-chih t'ung-chien*, 177, 5504 ff.–5510). At this point Kakhun omits about four lines in *HKSC*, 13, 523c.

372   了無火狀, in *HKSC*, 13, 523c26, makes more sense than 若無告狀.

373   Or 攝大乘論, by Asaṅga, brother of Vasubandhu. There are three Chinese translations: (1) by Buddhaśānta 佛陀扇多 (覺定) in 531 in 2 chapters (*KT*. 16, 1314a–1335b; *T*. 31, 97a–112b); (2) by Paramārtha of Liang between 563 and 564 in 3 chapters (*KT*. 16, 1104a–1132c; *T*. 31, 113b–132c); and (3) by Hsüan-tsang between 647 and 649 (*KT*. 16, 1336a–1364b; *T*. 31, 132c–152a). For Japanese studies on this work see Ui Hakuju, *Shōdaijōron no kenkyū* (Tokyo, 1935); Sasaki Gesshō 佐佐木月樵, *Kan'yaku shihon taishō, Shōdaijōron tsuki Chibetto yaku Shōdaijōron* 漢譯四本對照 攝大乘論附西藏譯攝大乘論 (Tokyo, 1959); and Suzuki Munetada 鈴木宗忠, "Shōdaijōron ni kansuru nisan no mondai," in *Yuishiki tetsugaku kenkyū* (Kyoto, 1957), pp. 141–168.

374   *SGSG*, 4, 9.

375   *Naema* was the eleventh rank in Silla (*SGSG*, 1, 5; 38, 1), the color of whose official robe was blue (*SGSG*, 33, 1). *SGSG*, 4, 9, reads Chemun 諸文 for Chebu.

376   The twelfth rank (*SGSG*, 1, 5; 38, 1); the color of the official robe was yellow (*SGSG*, 33, 1).

my duty to support you," the spirit replied; "you have an agreement with the sea dragon to erect a monastery, and now the dragon is here with me." The master then asked where the monastery should be built. The spirit replied, "North[377] of the Unmun 雲門, where a flock of magpies are pecking at the ground. That is the place." The following morning the master, together with the spirit and the dragon, went to the place and, after the ground was cleared, found the remains of a stone pagoda. A monastery (*saṅghārāma*) was erected there, named the Unmun monastery,[378] and there [the master] stayed.

The spirit continued to protect the master invisibly until one day he returned and said, "My end is drawing near, and I want to receive the Bodhisattva ordination[379] so that I can be qualified for eternity." The master administered the rites, and they vowed to save each other from endless transmigration.[380] Afterwards, [the master] asked if he might see the spirit's manifestation. The latter answered, "You may look to the east at dawn." [The master] then saw a big arm reach through the clouds to Heaven. The spirit spoke, "Now you have seen my arm. Although I possess supernatural power,[381] I still cannot escape mortality. I shall die on such and such a day in such and such a place, and I hope that you will come there to bid me farewell." The master went to the place as instructed and there saw an old black badger whimper and die. It was the spirit.

---

377 For 小 read 北, with *T* editors, for this at least makes more sense.

378 In *SGYS*, 4, 186, the master Poyang 寶壤, on his way home from China, encountered a dragon in the Western Sea which took him to the water palace, recited scriptures, presented him with a robe of golden gauze and one of his sons, Imok 璃目, to accompany him to Korea. The dragon then asked him to build a monastery at Chakkap 鵲岬, and it was therefore called the Chakkap monastery. Unmun is in North Kyŏngsang, about 96 *ri* east of Ch'ŏngdo (*TYS*, 26, 22b, 24b). The monastery was first built in 560 and repaired by Wŏn'gwang in 591; Koryŏ T'aejo granted it the name of Unmun sŏnsa 雲門禪寺 in 937 (*Kuksa taesajŏn*, II, 989a-b; *SGYS*, 4, 186). According to *CJS*, I, 356–363 (cf. *CKS*, I, 348–353), the monastery was first built by Wŏn'gwang and the construction was continued by Poyang and completed by the National Preceptor Wŏnŭng 圓應國師 (1052–1144). See *Misul charyo* 美術資料, 5 (1962), 11–14.

379 For a thorough consideration of this subject in a Western language see *HBGR*, pp. 142a–146b. *SGSG* and *SGYS* do not furnish information on this subject for the Silla period. For the Koryŏ period, however, *KRS* offers an abundance. The ordination was administered to the Koryŏ kings by the National or Royal Preceptor, normally on the fifteenth day of the sixth month. The first Koryŏ king to receive such ordination was Tŏkchong 德宗 in 1032 (*KRS*, 5, 25a), and the last, King Kongmin in 1352 (*KRS*, 38, 10a). For this see *CG*, 15 (1960), 22–23.

380 *SGYS*, 4, 183, reads: 結生生相濟之約.

381 *SGYS* has 雖有此身 for ———神.

A female dragon in the Western Sea used to attend the master's lectures. At that time there was a drought and the master asked her to make rain to alleviate disaster in the country. [The dragon] replied, "The supreme deity will not allow it. If I make rain without his permission, I sin against the deity and have no way of escaping punishment." The master said, "My power can save you from it." Immediately, the morning clouds appeared on the southern mountain[382] and rain poured down.[383] Thunder of Heaven broke out, indicating imminent punishment, and the dragon was frightened. The master hid her under his couch and continued to expound the scriptures. A heavenly messenger then appeared saying, "I was ordered by the supreme deity. You are the host of the fugitive. What shall I do if I am unable to carry out my orders?" The master, pointing to a pear tree in the garden, replied, "She has transformed herself into that tree. You may strike it." [The messenger] struck it and then left. The dragon then came out and thanked the master. Grateful to the tree that had suffered punishment for her sake, the dragon touched the trunk with her hand and the tree revived.[384]

In his thirtieth year (608) King Chinp'yŏng, troubled by frequent border raids by Ko[gu]ryŏ,[385] decided to ask help from Sui to retaliate and asked the master to draft the petition for a foreign campaign. The master replied, "To destroy others in order to preserve oneself is not the way of a monk (*śramaṇa*). But since I, a poor monk,[386] live in Your Majesty's territory and waste Your Majesty's clothes and food, I do not dare disobey." He then relayed the king's request [to Sui].

The master was detached and retiring by nature, but affectionate and loving to all. He always smiled when he spoke and never showed signs of anger. His reports, memorials, memoranda, and correspondence were all composed by himself and were greatly admired by the whole country. Power

---

382 朝隮: *Shih ching*, 151, 3 (Karlgren, pp. 96).

383 崇朝而雨: *Shih ching*, 51, 2 (Karlgren, p. 33).

384 The above episode is in *SGYS*, 4, 189, under Poyang and Imok. That the dragon can transform itself into a tree or become a tree demon is a commonplace. See M. W. de Visser, *The Dragon in China and Japan* (Amsterdam, 1913), pp. 15–16.

385 King Yŏngyang 嬰陽王 of Koguryŏ attacked Silla's borders in 603 and 608 (*SGSG*, 20, 2). Here the wording is slightly different from *SGSG*, 4, 10.

386 For 貧道 see, for example, *T.* 54, 251b ff. *SGSG*, 4, 10, reads 食大王之水草 for 費大王之衣食.

was bestowed on him so that he might govern the provinces,[387] and he used the opportunity to promote Buddhism, setting an example for future generations.

In the thirty-fifth year (613) an Assembly of One Hundred Seats[388] was held in the Hwangnyong monastery to expound the scriptures and harvest the fruits of blessing. The master headed the entire group. He used to spend days at Kach'wi monastery 加悉寺,[389] lecturing on the true way.

[1021b] Kwisan 貴山[390] and Ch'wihang 箒頂[391] from Saryang district 沙梁部[392] came to the master's door and, lifting up their robes,[393] respectfully said, "We are ignorant and without knowledge. Please give us a maxim which will serve to instruct us for the rest of our lives." The master replied, "There are ten commandments in the Bodhisattva ordination 菩薩戒.[394] But, since you are subjects and sons, I fear you cannot practice all of them. Now, here are five commandments for laymen:[395] serve your sovereign with loyalty;

---

387 *HKSC*, 13, 524a7, reads 一隅傾奉皆委以治方. Does it mean that the master was in charge of the clerics in the provinces? Because all ecclesiastical posts were military appointments in Silla (*SGSG*, 40, 10), this may have been a military office. See *Yŏksa hakpo*, 6 (1954), 183–186.

388 This was organized by the Sui envoy Wang Shih-i 王世儀 (*SGSG*, 4, 10). For more see n. 86 to the Introduction.

389 Situated north of Kasŭlgap 嘉瑟岬 and east of the Unmun monastery (*SGYS*, 4, 184). Kach'wi is the site of the monastery where Wŏn'gwang is said to have resided upon his return from T'ang.

390 The following is an almost verbatim quotation, with a few minor variants, from *SGSG*, 45, 7. Kwisan was the son of Muŭn 武殷. In 602, in a campaign against Paekche, he was ambushed by a large enemy army and died in action. King Chinp'yŏng granted him the posthumous title of *Naema*. See n. 375 above.

391 He also performed wonders of valor in the same campaign. King Chinp'yŏng honored him with the posthumous title of *Taesa*. See n. 376 above.

392 Formerly Kohŏ village 高墟村 in Tolsan 突山, one of the six villages of the ancient Silla confederation (*SGSG*, 1, 1); it became one of the six administrative districts in A.D. 32 with the name of Saryang pu (*SGSG*, 1, 5). See also *SGYS*, 1, 42, 43–44, and *KRS*, 57, 2a. For a study of the six villages and, especially, the location of Saryang pu see Suematsu, *Shiragi-shi no shomondai*, pp. 235–307; *SG*, 28 (1937), 82–125; *Yŏksa hakpo*, 1 (Pusan, 1952), 45–46; 17–18 (1962), 413–436.

393 摳衣: *Li-chi chu-su* 禮記注疏 (*SPPY*), 2, 1b (Couvreur, *Li Ki*, p. 17); cf. *K'ung-tzu chia-yu* 孔子家語 (*SPPY*), 1, 3b (R. P. Kramers, *K'ung Tzu Chia Yu: The School Sayings of Confucius* [Leiden, 1950], p. 207).

394 See n. 379 above.

395 世俗五戒. In connection with the five precepts of Wŏn'gwang and the way of the *hwarang*, we should mention a stone tablet, known as the *Imsin sŏgi sŏk* 壬申誓記石. The tablet was discovered in 1934 (or 1940, according to the *Seoul taehakkyo nonmunjip*, 5 [1957], 1) on the hill behind the site of the Sŏkchang monastery 石丈寺, near Kyŏngju, and is preserved in the Kyŏngju Museum. The inscription, consisting of seventy-four logographs in five lines (18, 16, 14, 16, and 10 respectively) and written in *hyangch'al* 鄉札, reads in part: "On the sixteenth day of the sixth month of the year

tend your parents with filial piety; treat your friends with sincerity; do not retreat from a battlefield; be discriminating about the taking of life. Exercise care in the performance of them." Kwisan said, "We accept your wishes with regard to the first four. But what is the meaning of being discriminating about the taking of life?" The master answered, "Not to kill during the months of spring and summer nor during the six maigre feast days is to choose the time.[396] Not to kill domestic animals such as cows, horses, chickens, dogs, and tiny creatures whose meat is less than a mouthful is to choose the creatures. Though you may have the need, you should not kill often.[397] These are the good rules for laymen." Kwisan and his friend adhered to them without ever breaking them.

Later, when the king was ill and no physician could cure him,[398] the master was invited to the palace to expound the Law and was here given separate quarters. While expounding the texts and lecturing on the truth, he succeeded in gaining the king's faith. At the first watch, the king and his courtiers saw that the master's head was as golden as the disk of the sun.[399] The king's illness was immediately cured.

When the master's monastic years were well advanced, he went to the inner court [of the palace] by carriage. The king personally took care of the master's clothing and medicine,[400] hoping thus to monopolize the rewards.

---

imsin, we two solemnly swear by Heaven to conduct ourselves with perfect loyalty and not to commit any fault for a span of three years. We swear that if we act contrary to this oath we will sin gravely against Heaven. Especially when the country is unstable we swear to translate the oath into practice. Previously, on the twenty-second day of the seventh month of the year *sinmi* 辛未, we pledged ourselves to master the *Book of Songs*, the *Book of Documents*, the *Rites*, and *the Tso chuan* in the like period of three years." The identity of the two is unknown, but they might have been Kwisan and Ch'wihang. Suematsu dates the tablet to 732, while Yi Pyŏng-do, because of the use of the *hyangch'al* system and the contents of the oath, puts it before 676, the year of the unification of the Three Kingdoms by Silla. A valuable record of contemporary facts, the tablet refers to such matters as the development of the *hyangch'al*, the growth of the *hwarang*, and the daily life of the upper class in Silla. The tablet is also unique in that it records a private oath rather than one of a public nature. See *Seoul taehakkyo nonmunjip*, 5 (1957), 1–7; Suematsu, *Shiragi-shi no shomondai*, pp. 451–465.

396 The eighth, fourteenth, fifteenth, twenty-third, twenty-ninth, and thirtieth days constitute the six monthly fast days. See *T.* 25, 159b–160c (Lamotte, II, 825, 826, and 827–828, n. 2).

397 Two missing logographs are reconstructed as 有 and 用 according to *SGYS*, 4, 184, line 2.

398 A lacuna after 不 is read 損 with *HKSC*, 13, 524a27, and *SGYS*, 4, 181.

399 *SGYS*, 4, 181, following *HKSC*, 13, 524a29–524b1, reads 金色晃然有象(像)日輪 for 金色如日輪. The *HKSC* version is slightly different from the one we have here.

400 *HKSC*, 13, 524a9, reads 藥食 for 藥石 ("medicine and the needle": *Lieh tzu*, 5, 14a [Graham, *The Book of Lien-tzu*, p. 106]).

Except for his monastic robe and begging bowl, the master gave away all the offerings bestowed upon him to the monasteries in order to glorify the true law and to lead both the initiated and uninitiated. When he was near the end, the king tended him in person. The king received the commission to transmit (*pariṇāmanā*)[401] the Dharma after the master's death and to save the people. Thereupon [the master] explained the omens to him in detail. In the fifty-eighth year of the era *kŏnbok* 建福 (640),[402] seven days after his illness, he died, sitting upright, in his residence, after giving his last commandments in a lucid, compassionate voice. In the sky northeast of the Hwangnyong monastery music filled the air, and an unusual fragrance pervaded the hall. The whole nation experienced grief mingled with joy. The burial materials and attending rites were the same as those for a king. He was ninety-nine years old. It was the fourth year of the era *chen-kuan* (640).[403]

Years later, a baby died in the womb. According to the popular belief that if it were buried beside the tomb of a virtuous man the family's descendants would not die out, the family of the dead baby buried it there secretly. The same day, the earth shook[404] and threw the baby corpse out of the tomb.

His reliquary on Samgi Mountain still stands today.

Wŏn'gwang's able disciple Wŏnan 圓安 was also a native of Silla. He was astute and quick-witted. He loved to travel and enjoyed plumbing the mysteries of the religion. He went north to Hwando 丸都[405] and east to Pullae 不耐.[406] Later, he also traveled in [the states of] Western Yen (384–395) and Northern Wei (386–534).[407] Upon arriving in the imperial capital he familiarized himself with local customs. He studied the scriptures and treatises, was versed

---

401 囑累 (*SH*, p. 489a).

402 Ninth year of Queen Sŏndŏk, rather than the fifty-eighth year of the era *kŏnbok*, which did not exist. *SGYS*, 4, 183, on the authority of the *Kobon sui chŏn*, says that he died at the age of eighty-four.

403 Should be the fourteenth year of *chen-kuan*.

404 Or "the lightning struck the corpse and threw it out of the tomb."

405 For 九都 read 丸都 (*YSGYS*, 4, 382, n. 2), the Koguryŏ capital for more than 200 years, from the 2d century to 427, when it was transferred to P'yŏngyang. For various theories on the location of the city see *Kuksa taesajŏn*, II, 1776a–b.

406 Pullae is modern Anbyŏn 安邊 in South Hamgyŏng. Formerly of the territory of East Ye 東濊, under Koguryŏ it was called Piyŏlhol 比烈忽 and under Silla, Piyŏl chu 比列州. King Kyŏng-dŏk changed its name to Sakchŏng kun 朔庭郡; under Koryŏ it was known as Tŭngju 登州 (*TYS*, 49, 1a–2a; *Wei chih*, 30, 1005a; *Han'guk sa*, I, 253–259, 326–327).

407 Western Yen and Northern Wei used here as metonymy for China. *HKSC*, 13 524a22, reads simply 西燕魏.

in their essence, and understood even their subtlest meanings clearly. He then followed the footsteps of his teacher Wŏn'gwang.[408] Because he was famed for his attainment of the Way, the *T'e-chin* 特進[409] Hsiao Yü 蕭瑀 (574–647)[410] had him reside in thd Chin-liang monastery 津梁寺 in Lan-t'ien 藍田[411] and provided him with the four necessaries.[412] We do not know his end.

[1021c] The eulogy says: Formerly the master Hui-yüan 慧遠 (334–416)[413] did not neglect worldly texts. During his lectures he illustrated his points by quotations from Chuang Tzu and Lao Tzu in order to make people understand the mysterious purports. Now, the commandments for laymen laid down by the master Wŏn'gwang were really the result of his all-embracing knowledge and demonstrated the efficacy of his technique of preaching the Dharma according to the receptivity of his listeners. Discrimination in the taking of life is none other than T'ang's 湯 leaving one side of the net open[414] and Confucius' not shooting at roosting birds.[415] As for his ability to move heavenly deities and dismiss heavenly messengers, he must have possessed unimaginable religious power.

---

408 光塵 might allude to 和光同塵 in *Tao te ching*, 4 and 56 (Waley, pp. 146, 210): "All glares tempered, all dust smoothed." See Kobayashi Shimmei 小林信明, "Wakōdōjin kō," in *Tōhōgakkai sōritsu jūgoshūnen kinen Tōhōgaku ronshū* 東方學會創立十五周年記念東方學論集 (Tokyo, 1962), pp. 105–115.

409 *Hou Han shu*, 4, 0658b; *Chin shu*, 24, 1147c; *Chiu T'ang shu*, 42, 3242b (des Rotours, I, 35): "an honorary title for an official of the senior second rank." Hsiao received this title in 635 (*Tzu-chih t'ung-chien*, 194, 6117).

410 For 肅 read 蕭, as in A24b4. Son of Emperor Hsiao-ming of the Later Liang (542–585; *BD*, 707) and brother of Hsiao Ts'ung. He served under Sui as well as the first two emperors of T'ang (*T'ang hui-yao* 唐會要 [*TSCC*], 1, 3). He espoused Buddhism and requested the emperor to turn his mansion into a monastery (*HTS*, 101, 3915a-b; *Chiu T'ang shu*, 63, 3304c–3305b; *KHMC*, 7, 135a; *BD*, 722). He died at the age of seventy-four.

411 Built in 621 (*HKSC*, 19, 587b22–23). For Lan-t'ien, southeast of Ch'ang-an in Shensi, see *Tu-shih fang-yü chi-yao*, 53, 2345 ff.

412 Clothing, victuals, bedding, and medicine. (*Ekottarāgama* 增一阿含經 13, *T*. 2, 610a13–14; *Samantapāsādika* 善見律毘婆沙 13, *T*. 24, 763b13–14).

413 *KSC*, 6, 357c-361c (Zürcher, I, 240–253); *BD*, 882; Watter Liebenthal, "Shih Hui-yüan's Buddhism as set forth in His Writings," *JAOS*, 70 (1950), 243–259; Kimura Eiichi, *ed.*, *Eon kenkyū* 慧遠研究 (2 vols.; Kyoto, 1960–1962) and Robinson, *Early Mādhyamika in India and China*. pp. 96–114, 196–205).

414 湯網去三面: *Shih chi*, 3, 0011b (*MH*, I, 180).

415 仲尼弋不射宿: *Analects*, VII, 26 (Waley, p. 128).

Anham

Sŏk Anham's 釋安含 secular name was Kim. He was a grandson of the poet [who held the rank of] Ich'an 伊湌.[416] Blessed with enlightenment at birth, he was by nature free of preconceptions and prejudices. He was resolute, and his magnanimity, profound and beautiful, was boundless. He traveled about as the fancy took him; he would observe local manners and make conversions on his own initiative. In the twenty-second year of King Chinp'yŏng (600),[417] in the company of an eminent monk, Hyesuk 惠宿,[418] he planned to sail to Nip'ojin 泥浦鎭, but they met with a storm near Sŏp Island 涉島[419] and were forced to return and moor their boat. The following year (601)[420] a royal decree permitted promising students to travel to China for study. The master was allowed to go; he sailed with a Silla envoy.

When he was received by the emperor, the latter was greatly pleased and installed him in the Ta-hsing-sheng monastery 大興聖寺.[421] Within a few months the master succeeded in understanding thoroughly the mysterious purport [of the Law]. Since the journey of ten stations from Mount Hua 華山 to Hsien-chang 仙掌[422] is completed in less than a day, who hears the even-

---

416 Or Ich'ŏkch'an 伊尺湌, the second of the seventeen ranks in Silla established in A.D. 32 (*SGSG*, 38, 1).

417 Not entered in *SGSG*; *SGYS*, 3, 132, has a passing reference to his image enshrined in the Golden Hall of the Hŭngnyun monastery.

418 A member of the *hwarang* who lived in the village of Chŏksŏn 赤善村 (Chŏkkok 赤谷 in An'g-ang hyŏn; *SGYS*, 4, 189; *SGSG*, 34, 5–6) for some twenty years. One day, upon seeing Knight Kudam 瞿旵 eating the meat of some game he had hunted, he cut off a piece of flesh from his own thigh and gave it to the knight as a sign of his stern disapproval. He was buried east of I hyŏn 耳縣. The Hyesuk monastery in An'gang is said to have been his abode. His image is also found in the Golden Hall of the Hŭngnyun (*SGYS*. 3, 132; 4, 189; 5, 218). According to the last reference, he built the Amitābha monastery.

419 It does not appear on the sea routes between China and Silla during the T'ang era (see Naitō Shunpo, *Chōsen-shi kenkyū*, pp. 367–480).

420 Not entered in *SGSG*, 4.

421 In the southwest corner of T'ung-i ward in Ch'ang-an, the residence of T'ang Kao-tsu before his enthronement; in 627 (or 629, according to the *KHMC*, 28, 329c) it became a monastery. See *Ch'ang-an chih* 長安志, 9, 9a, in *Tōdai kenkyū no shiori*, 6 (1956); *T.* 49, 363c9–10; and *Ta-T'ang nei-tien lu* 大唐內典錄 5, *T.* 55, 280c6–7.

422 In Hua-yin hsien, Shensi; called "Fairy Palm" because strange rocks of Mount Hua soar above the clouds (*Chung-kuo ku-chin ti-ming ta-tz'u-tien*, p. 936d).

ing drum? Since the land of a thousand leagues between the Ch'in Range 秦嶺[423] and Ti-kung 帝宮 is covered overnight, who awaits the morning bell?[424] In five years Anham had absorbed the meditation in ten stages[425] and also the profound meaning of the [*Fa-hua*] *hsüan-i* 法華玄義[426]. In the twenty-seventh year (605)[427] the master returned to his country with the monk P'i-mo-chen-ti 毘摩眞諦 of Khotan[428] and the monk Nung-chia-t'o 農伽陀.[429]

---

[423] The Ch'in (or Nan-shan) Range runs from east of Kao-lan in Kansu midway between the Yellow, Wei, Han, and Kai rivers in the south of Shensi to Shen hsien of Honan. The mountain which specifically bears this name runs from T'ien-shui in Kansu to Shen hsien in Honan (*Chung-kuo ku-chin ti-ming ta-tz'u-tien*, p. 745c).

[424] The translation of the above allusion-packed passages is tentative. Kakhun is trying to state metaphorically the swiftness and agility of Anham's movements and the keenness of his intelligence, but I am not sure whether I have rendered the passages correctly.

[425] 十乘祕法: T'ien-t'ai mode of meditation in ten vehicles or stages for the attainment of bodhi. See *Mo-ho chih-kuan* 摩訶止觀 5A, *T.* 46, 52b1–4 (*MCB*, 12 [1962], 330–331).

[426] Or *Miao-fa lien-hua ching hsüan-i* (*T.* 33, 681a–814a). According to Satō Tetsuei 佐藤哲英, "Hokke gengi no seiritsu katei ni kansuru kenkyū," in *Indogaku bukkyōgaku kenkyū* 印度學佛教學研究, 6 (1958), 312–322, Chih-i 智顗 (538–597) lectured on the profound meaning of the *Lotus* sūtra twice in his life: first when he was in the Wa-kuan monastery in Chin-ling (568–575) and again when he was in Ching-chou (Chiang-ling) in 593. No lecture notes survive of the first. As for the second, our sources are silent about the place of the lecture. The Prince of Ch'in (later Sui Yang-ti) did not grant the Yü-ch'üan monastery 玉泉寺 its plaque until the twenty-third day of the seventh month of 593, and a request signed by Hui-yen 彗巖 and Ch'en Tzu-hsiu 陳子秀 for a lecture on the *Lotus* is dated the tenth day of the eighth month of the same year (*T.* 46, 801a). In view of these facts, Satō thinks that the second lecture must have taken place after the tenth day of the eighth month at the Yü-ch'üan monastery. If it had been delivered before that date, as some propose, it must have been at a monastery other than Yü-ch'üan. Kuan-ting 灌頂 (561–632) edited the notes between 595 and 597 and he presented them in the autumn of 597 to his master on the T'ien-t'ai mountain. After the master's death he worked on a revision, which probably was completed by the summer of 602. Hsüan-lang 玄朗 (673–754) may have rephrased the difficult passages around 748. With the compilation of notes, the *Fa-hua hsüan-i shih-ch'ien* 法華玄義釋籤 (764), by Chan-jan 湛然 (711–782), the text of the *Fa-hua hsüan-i* was firmly established. For the organization of this text see *MCB*, 12 (1962), 206–214.

[427] Not entered in *SGSG*. Ch'oe Ch'i-wŏn, a few lines below, proposes 625 instead.

[428] In southwest Sinkiang, about 2,500 miles west of Korea. For notices in Chinese sources see *Ch'ien Han shu*, 96A, 0606c; *Hou Han shu*, 118, 0904c–d (Chavannes [4], 171–174); *Pei shih*, 97, 3041b–c (Chavannes [2], 393, n. 9); *Chiu T'ang shu*, 198, 3613c; *Chou shu*, 50, 2341a (Roy Andrew Miller, *Accounts of Western Nations in the History of the Northern Chou Dynasty* [Berkeley and Los Angeles, 1959], pp. 10–11); *HTS*, 221A, 4153a (Édouard Chavannes, *Documents sur les Tou-kiue* [*turcs*] *occidentaux* [Paris, n.d.], pp. 125–128). For a detailed study see Pelliot (8), pp. 408–425, and Sir Aurel Stein, *Ancient Khotan* (2 vols.; Oxford, 1907). For Khotanese Buddhism see Hatani, *Saiiki no bukkyō*, pp. 235–307, 324–346.

[429] I cannot identify him.

This was the first time that foreign monks from Serindia[430] came directly to Kyerim 雞林.[431]

In the biography of Ŭisang 義湘, Ch'oe Ch'i-wŏn said: "Ŭisang was born in the forty-second year of the era *kŏnbok* of King Chinp'yŏng (635).[432] In the same year the eastern sage, the master of the Law Anhong 安弘, came from T'ang with two masters of the Tripiṭaka[433] from the West as well as two Chinese monks." A note says: "P'i-mo-chen-ti from Udyāna 烏萇國[434]

---

430 See Fujita Toyohachi 藤田豊八, *Tōzai kōshōshi no kenkyū: Saiiki hen* 東西交涉史の研究, 西域篇 (Tokyo, 1943), pp. 352–359; Shiratori Kurakichi, *MTB*, 15 (1956), 73–176.

431 Originally called Sirim 始林, referring to the forest of Kyerim in Kyŏngju. According to *SGSG*, 1, 7, and 34, 1, in the third month of A.D. 65 King T'arhae 脫解王, the fourth ruler of Silla, heard at night the crying of a cock west of the capital, in the vicinity of Sirim, and sent Hogong 瓠公 to investigate. The latter found, hanging from a branch of a tree, a golden box and beneath it a white cock. He thought it strange and reported the matter to the king, who had him bring the box and open it. Inside was a beautiful child. The king thought the boy a gift from Heaven and reared him. As the boy grew, he became more sagacious and wise. He was therefore named Alchi 閼智, and because he had come from the golden box, he took the surname Kim. He changed the name of Sirim to Kyerim, making it the name of his country. On the other hand, *SGYS*, 1, 44–45, reports that Hyŏkkose 赫居世, the founder of Silla, was born at Kyejŏng 雞井 and that because of the appearance of the Kyeryongsŏ 雞龍瑞 at the time of the birth of Queen Aryŏng 閼英 the country was named Kyerim. It is said that Silla began to be called Kyerim when, in 663, T'ang Kao-tsung named it Kyerimju todokpu 雞林州都督府 and King Munmu, *Kyerimju todok* 雞林州都督 (according to *SGSG*, 6, 3, this took place in the fourth month [May 13–June 10]). Contemporary Chinese histories record Saro, but not Kyerim; indeed, Kyerim seems to have been a Silla invention. *SGYS*, 4, 188, says that Korea was known to India as the country of the cock, basing its information on I-ching's gloss in *Nan-hai chi-kuei nei-fa-chuan* 南海寄歸內法傳, 1, *T*. 54, 206a (Takakusu, *A Record of the Buddhist Religion as Practised in India and the Malay Archipelago by I-Tsing* [Oxford, 1896], p. 17), where it reads: "Those who respect the cocks are the people of Korea, which is called in India Kukkteśvara, *Khukuta* meaning 'cock' and *īśvara*, 'honorable.' People in India say that that country honors cocks as gods, and therefore people wear wings on their heads as an ornamental sign." See Charles Haguenauer, "Le 'ki-kouei' 雞貴 de Yi-tsing et le 'kye-rim' de l'histoire," *Kano kyōju kanreki kinen Shinagaku ronsō* 狩野教授還曆記念支那學論叢 (Kyoto, 1928), pp. 13–25; Cho Chi-hun, "Silla kukho yŏn'gu non," in *Koryŏ taehakkyo osip chunyŏn kinyŏm nonmunjip* 高麗大學校五十周年記念論文集 (1955), pp. 167–188; Son Chin-t'ae 孫晉泰, "China minjok ŭi unggye sinang kwa kŭ chŏnsŏl," *CH*, 3 (1935), 76–92; and *SR*, 18 (1933), 453–464, on Sirim 始林.

432 *SGYS*, 4, 194 ff. (*JAOS*, 82 [1962], 56), to which add Yaotani Takayasu 八百谷孝保, "Shiragisō Gishō-den kō," *Shina bukkyō shigaku* 支那佛教史學 3 (1939), 79–94, and *Wŏnjong mullyu*, 22, 419c-d and 429c. This is the biography of Ŭisang mentioned also by Hyŏngnyŏn Chŏng 赫連挺 (*KRS*, 11, 24b; 12, 17a), the author of the *Kyunyŏ chŏn* (1075). See *SGYS*, Appendix, p. 56 (*Asiatische Studien*, 11 [1957–1958], 47–48).

433 A25b3 and *CPT*, I, 63, read 三藏, "with three Masters of the Tripiṭaka."

434 Or 烏仗那 and 烏茶 (Walter Fuchs, "Huei-ch'ao's Pilgerreise durch Nordwest-Indien und Zentral-Asien um 726," in *Sitzungsberichte der Preussischen Akademie der Wissenschaften*, 30 [Berlin, 1938], 446–447); 烏長 in *Wang o ch'ŏnch'ukkuk chŏn* 往五天竺國傳 in *SGYS*, Appendix, p. 24). Northwest of Kashmir. "A kingdom of the upper Indus valley, probably modern Swat," says Need-

in northern India was forty-four years old. Nung-chia-t'o was forty-six years old. Buddhasaṅga 佛陀僧伽 from the country of Mathurā 摩豆羅國[435] was also forty-six years old. They had traversed fifty-two countries before arriving in China. They finally reached Korea, where they stayed in the Hwangnyong monastery and translated the *Chan-t'an hsiang-huo hsing-kuang miao-nü ching* 栴檀香火星光妙女經,[436] which was noted down by a native monk, Tamhwa 曇和.[437] Soon afterwards the Chinese monks memorialized the king, requesting permission to return [home]. The king granted them their leave and had them escorted on the trip." From this account it is clear that Anhong must have been the master (*Upādhyāya*).'

According to the *Annals of Silla* 新羅本記, however, in the thirty-seventh year of King Chinhŭng (576) Anhong went to Ch'en in order to seek the Law and returned [1022a] with two foreign monks, including P'i-mo-chen-ti.[438] [Anhong] brought back the *Laṅkāvatāra*[439] and *Śrīmālā* [*siṁhanāda*] sūtras 勝鬘經[440] and also Buddha relics. But a span of almost fifty years separates the end of the reign of King Chinhŭng from the era *kŏnbok* of King Chinp'yŏng. How could this be so, when the three masters of the Tripiṭaka had not even been there yet? Perhaps Anham and Anhong were actually two different persons; however, the [three] masters of the Tripiṭaka who ac-

ham, *Science and Civilization in China*, I, 209. See also Luciano Petech, *Northern India According to the Shui-ching-chu* (Rome, 1950), p. 9; Chavannes (2), 407, n. 2; Beal, *Si Yu Ki*. I, 119–135; Sir Aurel Stein, *Serindia* (Oxford, 1921), I, 5–20; Watters, *On Yuan Chwang's Travels in India*, I, 225 ff.

435 Southwest of modern Jumna. The place is identified with Maholi, 5 miles southwest of the present Mathura (Muttra) (Bimala Churn Law, *Geography of Early Buddhism* [London, 1932], pp. 20–21). Beal, I, 179–183; Watters, I, 301–313.

436 Does this refer to *Chan-t'an hsiang-shen t'o-lo-ni ching* 栴檀香身陀羅尼經, translated by Fa-hsien of Sung in 1001 in one chapter (*T*. 21,906a-b)? There is a *dhāranī* called 栴檀香身 and if one recites it one can see Avalokiteśvara and cure diseases (*Fo-hsüeh ta-tz'u-tien*, p. 181a). See also *BKD*, VI, 334d–335a.

437 Otherwise unknown.

438 He "went to Sui and returned with two monks, including P'i-mo-lo" (*SGSG*, 4, 7).

439 There are three translations: (1) by Guṇabhadra of Liu-Sung in 443 in 4 chapters (*KT*. 10, 785a–830b; *T*. 16, 480a–514b); (2) by Bodhiruci in 513 in 10 chapters (*KT*. 10, 831a–917a; *T*. 16. 514c–586b); and (3) by Śikṣānanda between 700 and 704 in 7 chapters (*KT*. 10, 919a–982a; *T*. 16, 587a–640c). See D.T. Suzuki, *Studies in the Laṅkāvatāra Sūtra* (London, 1930).

440 The full title is: 勝鬘獅子吼一乘大方便方廣經. Translated by Guṇabhadra (394–468) between 435 and 443 in one chapter (*KT*. 6, 1361a–1370a; *T*. 12, 217a–223b). See also Ui Hakuju, "Shōmangyō no bonbun danpen," in *Nagoyadaigaku bungakubu jisshūnen kinen ronshū* 名古屋大學文學部十周年記念論集 (1954), pp. 189–210; Kagawa Yoshio 香川孝雄, "Shōmangyō no kenkyū," *Bukkyō daigaku kenkyū kiyō* 佛教大學研究紀要 32 (1956), 47–82.

companied them bore the same names. Since the names are the same, I have
written their biographies in combination. As for the [three] masters of the
Tripiṭaka from Serindia, we do not know whether they stayed or departed, or
how they ended their lives.

After the master returned to his country, he composed a book of prognostication,[441] the prints of which subsequently fell into disorder, making it
difficult to guess who the author was. The meaning [of the prognostication]
is equally obscure, and the reader finds it difficult to understand. For instance
we find sentences like "the bird ulūka[442] . . . disperses," or "the first princess
will be buried in Trāyastriṁśa."[443] As for entries like "the defeat of a large
army stretching a thousand leagues," "the completion of the Four-Deva
monastery," "the time of the prince's return to his native land," or "the year
of prosperity under a powerful sovereign," though these are evasive and
remote prophecies, they sound as if he [the author] had seen their fulfillment with his very own eyes, without a single error.

On the twenty-third day of the ninth month of the ninth year of Queen
Sŏndŏk 善德女王[444] (October 13, 640), Anham died in the Mansŏn monastery
(*bodhi-maṇḍa*) 萬善道場[445] at the age of sixty-two. In the same month a
returning envoy from China met on the way the master of the Law, who was
sitting squarely on the green waves, joyfully heading westward. This is truly
what is meant by "soaring into the sky as if ascending a stairway and walking
on the water as if treading on the ground."

A certain Hallim scholar, Sŏl 薛,[446] by royal order compiled an epitaph

---

441 *SGYS*, 3, 139, mentions Anhong's *Tongdo sŏngnip ki* 東都成立記, but whether the book
contained any prognostication is uncertain. The contents of the *Haedong Anhong ki* 海東安弘記,
quoted in *KRS*, 57, 55a, are equally uncertain.

442 For this bird see *T.* 54, 584a, 612c, 636b, 660c, 669a, 773c, etc.; also E. H. Schafer, "The
Auspices of T'ang," *JAOS*, 83 (1963), 221, where it is identified as "the Eastern Nightjar, night-
hawk, or goatsucker," "a nocturnal, insectivorous, and ghostly bird."

443 切利天 or 三十三天: the second of the god-worlds of the Sphere of Desire (*Kāmadhātu*),
situated on the top of Mount Sumeru. On the summit lives Indra, and eight devas live on each side,
hence thirty-three devas altogether (*BHSD*, p. 257b).

444 Not entered in *SGSG*. We recall that this is the year in which Wŏn'gwang died.

445 "Platform (terrace, seat) of enlightenment"; the name given to the spot under the bodhi tree
on which the Buddha sat when he became enlightened. For how its meaning evolved in China from the
Northern Wei through Sui and T'ang see *HJAS*, 8 (1945), 309–311.

446 Perhaps referring to Sŏl Ch'ong 薛聰, though none of his writings are extant execpt a few
passages quoted in *SGSG*, 46, 5.

whose inscription reads: "The queen was buried in Trāyastriṁśa, and the Deva monastery was built. A strange bird cried at night, and a mass of soldiers died at dawn. The prince crossed the passes and had an audience with an emperor. He was beyond the frontier for five years, and he returned when he was thirty. The ups and downs of life are like a turning wheel. How can one avoid the distinction between self and not-self? At the age of sixty-two An-ham died at the Mansŏn monastery. On the sea the returning envoy met the master, who was sitting squarely on the waves and disappeared toward the West."[447] (Ten logographs on the slab are eroded and four or five more are unclear. The author takes what is legible and reconstructs the text by surmise.) This was probably nothing more than the trace of the deceased.

The eulogy says: The master's supernatural power *(abhijñā)*[448] and deliverance and freedom of movement were only a few signs of the great bodhisattva. The ordinary pen or mouth cannot exhaust them. After going to China and meeting the three monks from Serindia, he opened up a fountain of truth. Blowing the conch of the Law and showering the rain of the Law, his teaching, like a river, moistened the dried corner of the seashore. Indeed, he was a sage who propagated the Law.[449] A logograph [like] *o* 烏, after being copied three times, can become *ma* 馬.[450] I suspect that between *ham* 含 and *hong* 弘 one or the other must be a mistake.

---

447   This opaque prophecy, when punctuated correctly, is in a four-word rhymed verse. For instance, 還 (*g'wan*) 顏 (ngan); and 轉 (*tiwan*) 免 (*mian*) 善 (*dian*). Incomplete rhymes indicate corruption or omission by a copyist.

448   See Har Dayal, *The Bodhisattva Doctrine in Buddhist Sanskrit Literature*, pp. 106–134.

449   Omit 字 in 聖人字也, as in A26b9.

450   Other examples of the fallibility of the scribe are: *lu* 魯 for *yü* 魚 and *hsü* 虛 (or *ti* 帝) for *hu* 虎 (*Pao-p'u tzu* 抱朴子 [*WYWK*], 19, 381; repeated in *I-lin* 意林 [Taipei, 1959], 4, 17b) and *shih* 豕 for *hai* 亥 (*K'ung-tzu chia-yu* [*SPPY*], 9, 1a-b). Cf. Conrad H. Rawski, *Petrarch: Four Dialogues for Scholars* (Cleveland, 1967), pp. 34–36.

Āryavarman

Sŏk Āryavarman 釋阿離耶跋摩, possessed of supernal wisdom, was self-enlightened. His figure and features were unusual. When he first came to China from Silla in order to seek out a good teacher and study under him, there was no distance he would not go. He gazed down and rested in the dark valleys;[451] he climbed up and approached the heavens. He was determined not only to set a standard for his contemporaries but also to save the coming generations. He was eager to travel and observe and never ceased to go to remote places. At last he went to seek the Law in western India and climbed the distant Pamirs.[452] He searched for rare and wonderful scenes and witnessed all the sacred traces. His long-cherished desire was finally fulfilled. During this time, his funds [1022b] and food being exhausted, he stayed at the Nālanda monastery.[453] Soon thereafter, he died.

At the same time, an eminent [monk],[454] Hyeŏp 惠業, was staying in the Bodhi monastery, while [the eminent monks] Hyŏn'gak 玄恪 and Hyŏnjo 玄照 were at the Mahābodhi monastery 大覺寺.[455] These four completed their journey during the era *chen-kuan*, laid the foundations of a good cause, and swelled the monastic order. Taking leave of their native country, they went to observe Indian manners. They gained soaring reputations in both east and west and left behind an undying model. Had they not been superior personages endowed with great minds, how could they have expected to achieve this

---

451 Professor Robinson writes: "This is the image of the stargazer who sits down in a well and sees the stars in the daytime; metaphor for the yogin traveling in trance or the scholar traveling in his imagination."

452 For Hyech'o's account of the Pamirs see Fuchs, "Huei-ch'ao's Pilgerreise," pp. 455–456, and *MTB*, 16 (1957), 1–34.

453 North of Rājagṛha, capital of Magadha in central India. Kumāragupta I (*ca.* 413–455) probably founded the monastic community of Nālandā which soon became the center of Buddhist studies. Hsüan-tsang stayed there from 637 to 643 and I-ching from 676 to 685. The former interprets the name *nālanda* to mean *na-alanda* ("untiring generosity," *T*. 50, 714c); the latter terms it the name of a dragon. For the detailed description of the monastery by I-ching see Chavannes (1), pp. 84–98.

454 A lacuna of one logograph after "eminent" is conjectured to be "monk." For 專 read 惠 with A27b6.

455 North of the bodhi tree (*T*. 51, 918b6 ff.: Beal, II, 133–136).

much? According to the chronology, they may have departed for India at the same time as the master Hsüan-tsang 玄奘 (602–664),[456] but we do not know the exact year.

---

[456] He was in India between 629 and 645. For the translations of his *Ta-T'ang hsi-yü chi* 大唐西域記 (646) see Stanislas Julien, *Voyages de Pèlerins Bouddhistes* (vols. II. III; Paris, 1853–1858); Watters, *On Yuan Chwang's Travels in India*; Samuel Beal, *Si-yu-ki, Buddhist Records of the Western World* (2 vols.; London, 1906); for an annotated Japanese edition, Adachi Kiroku, *Daitō saiiki ki* (Kyoto, 1942–1943). For Buddhist sites described by him see Stein, *Ancient Khotan*, I, 223–235, 443 ff.; for his itinerary in Afghanistan, Alfred Foucher, in *Études Asiatiques publiées à l'occasion du vingt-cinquième anniversaire de l'École Française d'Extrême-Orient*, 1 (1925), 257–284. For his biography see *T*. 50, 214a–220c and 200c–280a; Arthur Waley, *The Real Tripitaka* (London, 1952), pp. 11–130; René Grousset, *In the Footsteps of the Buddha* (London, 1932), pp. 270 ff.

Hyeŏp

Sŏk Hyeŏp 釋惠(慧)業 was a vessel serene and profound, a man of solid substance in spiritual matters. His deportment was as impressive as a precipitous
crag, his manner neat and clear-cut.[457] Early in life he bade farewell to his
remote country and went directly to the Middle Kingdom. During the era
chen-kuan he traveled to the Western Regions. He traversed the vast desert
of moving sands and climbed the steep ridges of the Himālayas 雪嶺. When
the early sun heralded the dawn, he would lie down in the forest to rest.
When the bright moon flooded the firmament, he would then suffer the hardships of an endless journey. He took his life lightly for the sake of the Law,
his only ambition being its propagation. At last he went to the Bodhi monastery
and made a pilgrimage to witness the sacred traces. He then stayed in the
Nālanda monastery. After a while he begged leave to read the *Vimalakīrtinirdeśa*
淨明經,[458] compared it with the T'ang translation, and expounded it thoroughly and systematically. The marginalia to the *Liang lun* 梁論[459] reads: "A
Silla monk, Hyeŏp, copied it under the Buddha's toothwood tree (*Dantakāṣṭha*
佛齒樹)."[460] According to the [*Ch'iu-fa*] *chuan*, [Hye]ŏp died in the Nālanda
monastery in his sixties. What he copied in Sanskrit is still in the monastery.

---

457 For 戌削 see Takigawa Kametarō 瀧川龜太郎, *Shiki kaichū kōshō* 史記會注考證, IX (1933),
54; *Wen hsüan*, 7, 82 (von Zach, I, 105).

458 The three principal extant translations are: (1) by Chih Ch'ien (c. 223–253) in 2 chapters
(*KT*. 9, 1007a–1033b; *T*. 14, 519a–536c); (2) by Kumārajīva in 3 chapters (*KT*. 9, 977a–1006a;
T. 14, 537a–557b); and (3) by Hsüan-tsang in 6 chapters (*KT*. 9, 1035a–1080c; *T*. 14, 557c–588a).
A partial translation by Izumi Hōkei appeared in *The Eastern Buddhist*, 2 (1922–1923), 358–366;
3 (1924–1925), 55–69, 138–153, 224–242, 336–349; and 4 (1926–1928), 48–55, 177–190, 348–
366. The complete translation based on the Tibetan *Kanjur* is that by Étienne Lamotte, *L'Enseignement de Vimalakīrti* (Louvain, 1962). For Japanese studies see Kasuga Reichi, *Tōhō gakuhō*, 12 (Kyoto,
1942), 76–114, and Hashimoto Hōkei 橋本芳契, *Yuimagyō no shisōteki kenkyū* 維摩經の思想的研究
(Kyoto, 1966).

459 Or 梁攝論. According to Adachi, *Daitō saiiki guhō kōsōden* (Tokyo, 1942), p. 41, n. 1, this
refers to Paramārtha's translations of the *Mahāyānasaṃgraha* and to Vasubandhu's *She-ta-ch'eng-lun
shih* 攝大乘論釋 (*KT*. 16, 1149a–1313b; *T*. 31, 153c–270b). See also n. 373 above.

460 "Chewing stick of willow" (*T*. 51, 860b5–6; Herbert A. Giles, *The Travels of Fa Hsien* [Cam-
bridge, 1923], p. 29) or "Buddha's toothwood tree" (*T*. 54, 208c–209a; Takakusu, *A Record of the
Buddhist Religion*, p. 34). Takakusu defines it as "bits of sweet-smelling wood or root, or creeper,
the ends of which were to be masticated as a dentifrice, [but] not rubbed on the teeth." See *HJAS*,
9 (1947), 291, n. 186.

Hyeryun

Sŏk Hyeruyn 釋惠(慧)輪 was a native of Silla. His name in Sanskrit was Prajñāvarman 般若跋摩, in Chinese, Hyegap 惠(慧)甲.[461] From the time that he went forth from his family to become a monk in his country he had yearned for the holy land. Finally, he sailed to Min and Yüeh,[462] and from there walked to Ch'ang-an. He suffered cold and heat and experienced all manner of hardships.[463] Then, by imperial order, he went to the West as an attendant to the master of the Law Hyŏnjo. On the way they used scaling ladders to connect precipices.[464] Upon their arrival in India they made a pilgrimage to [witness the] miraculous traces [of the Buddha]. [Hyeryun] then stayed in the Cincāvihāra [monastery] 信者寺[465] in the country of Āmrāvatī 菴摩羅波國[466] for about ten years. Later he moved further east and lived in the Gandhārachanda monastery 犍陀羅山荼寺,[467] so rich in its property and products and so abundant in its offerings and feasts that it lacked nothing. Most of the foreign monks from the north [Serindia] usually stayed there, gathering like bees and clouds and each studying in his own discipline.

[Hye]ryun knew Sanskrit well and studied thoroughly[468] the [Abhidharma] kośa 俱舍.[469] "At the time of my return [to China], he was still alive, about forty years of age." Everything is exactly like the account in the *Ch'iu-fa kao-seng chuan* by the master of the Tripiṭaka, I-ching.

---

461 Chavannes (1), p. 79, n. 4. I-ching writes 慧 for 惠.

462 In the general area of modern Fukien. Cf. *Shih chi*, 114, 0252d f. (Watson, II, 251–254); Léonard Aurousseau, *BEFEO*, 23 (1923), 196 ff., 257–259.

463 This sentence is not in I-ching's biography.

464 I.e., they braved rugged peaks. This sentence is not in I-ching.

465 See *Ta-T'ang hsi-yü chi* 7, *T*. 51, 909c (Beal, II, 75).

466 Buddha, in one of his previous births as a brahmin youth named Sumedha, was born in that city. Identified with the modern city of Amaraoti close to the rivers of Dharanikotta (Law, *Geography of Early Buddhism*, p. 62; Chavannes [1], p. 18, n. 4).

467 Chavannes (1), p. 80, n. 4.

468 For 閑, meaning 習, see *Mencius*, IIIB, 8 (Legge, II, 283) and *Shih ching*, 127, 3 (Karlgren, pp. 81–82).

469 Synopsis of *Abhidharmamahāvibhāṣā* (compiled *ca*. 100–150 in Kashmir, translated by Hsüan-tsang in 200 chapters [*T*. 27, no. 1545]), compiled by Vasubandhu (*ca*. 450) and translated by Louis de la Vallée Poussin, *L'Abhidharmakośa de Vasubandhu* (Louvain, 1923–1931). This synopsis was also translated by Hsüan-tsang between 651 and 654 in 30 chapters (*T*. 29, la–159b) and became the principal text of the Chü-she school.

Hyŏn'gak

Sŏk Hyŏn'gak 釋玄恪 was a native of Silla. His moral power was unbending, and his wisdom and insight were great. He loved to lecture and preach, sensing a desire for his presence, and always fit [his discourse to] the capacities of his listeners. His contemporaries called him "a lotus in the fire".[470]

He used to complain of the fact that he had been born in a remote region and thus could not witness the glory of China. Upon hearing the news of China, he rejoiced and was able to cross over to China by boat.[471] [1022c] Scanning the T'ang capital, he felt discouraged, for he realized that he had already used up half his life span. But he resolved to seek out great masters and study under them.[472] Like the movement of the moon, day and night he went where his travels took him. Now he crossed over boulders heaped high where the courses of the birds were as high as the clouds;[473] now he traversed ice that extended for a thousand leagues, walking on the wind and lying down in the clouds.

At last he accompanied the master of the Law Hyŏnjo 玄照 and reached the Mahābodhi monastery in India. They traveled along the road of flaming fire and admired the "Shadowless Country" 無影之邦.[474] Carrying a writing

---

470 *T.* 14, 550b4 (Lamotte, *L'Enseignement de Vimalakīrti*, p. 298).

471 木道 from *Chou i*, 4, 13b–14a (Wilhelm, I, 173). See also Wilhelm, II, 244–245. *CPT*, III, 204, reads 水道. This term also occurs in the *Taegak kuksa munjip*, 6, 5a, and *woejip*, 12, 13b (*CKS*, I, 311–312).

472 In the original 敻目東圻, 遂含西笑, 心慚中晝. There is a parallel passage in *Taegak kuksa munjip*, 5, 9a5, which goes 敻自東睉, 素含西笑. A28a9–10 has 自 for 目, 晝 for 晝. Professor Chow's version reads: Looking high above and far away, he tried to see the eastern border of the T'ang domain and felt consoled by smiling toward the West. He regretted that he had not been enlightened with the bright clarity which characterizes high noon, but resolved to seek out great masters and study under them. His travels were like the movement of the moon, which turns at midnight following the natural course. For 西笑 see Huan T'an 桓譚, *Hsin lun* 新論 (Chih-hai 指海 ed.), 9b; 人聞長安樂, 則出門西向相笑, 肉味美, 對屠門而嚼: A man who heard that Ch'ang-an was a place of pleasure felt satisfied by walking out of his door and smiling toward the west; a man who heard that meat was delicious felt satisfied by facing the gate of the butcher shop and chewing.

473 鳥道: *Ri Haku no sakuhin* 李白の作品, in *Tōdai kenkyū no shiori*, 3, 2a (Shigeyoshi Obata, *The Works of Li Po* [Tokyo, 1935], p. 111).

474 無影之邦 is a metaphor for India. *KSC*, 7, 368a13–17, records a conversation between Ho Ch'eng-t'ien 何承天 (370–447) and Hui-yen 慧嚴 (364–443): "Ho Ch'eng-t'ien of Tung-hai had a great name for his works on natural phenomena. One day he asked [Hui-] yen what calendar was used in Buddha's country. [Hui-] yen replied, 'In India at the summer solstice the sun is in the center of

case, he delved into his studies, improved and polished [his learning],[475] and finally established himself as a master. After passing the age when "he no longer suffered from perplexities,"[476] he died from illness.

Hyŏnjo[477] was also an eminent monk of Silla. He and [Hyŏn'] gak passed the examination together and all through their lives they were of one mind. The place of his death is unknown.

There were two other Silla monks, whose names are unknown, who sailed from Ch'ang-an and reached the country of Śrībuja 室利佛逝國.[478] Both died of illness.

---

the [four] quarters and casts no shadows. This is what is called "Mid-Heaven" and has the virtue of Earth among the Five Elements. Its color is yellow, and this earth weighs twelve [of yours]. The year begins with *chien-ch'en* 建辰' " (i.e., chien-hsing, π^- *Sagittarii* and neighboring fainter stars [Schlegel, *Uranographie Chinoise*, p. 547]; i.e., *hsing-chi* 星記, the second of the twelve astronomical [non-astrological] *tz'u* 次). The first statement made by Hui-yen is entirely correct for those parts of India near the equator, where the sun at the summer solstice will be near the zenith and will cast no shadows. Hui-yen was therefore concerned to claim for India a central place in the cosmos, which is why he refers to the central yellow element, Earth. I owe the translation of the above passages and the explanation of them to Professor Joseph Needham.

475 琢玉: *Shih ching*, 55, 1 (Karlgren, p. 37). For 成器 see *Chou i*, 8, 4b (Wilhelm, I, 168–169, 365).

476 That is, forty years of age; reference to the *Analects*, II, 4 (Waley, p. 88).

477 According to I-ching, he was originally from T'ai-chou 太州 (Chavannes [1], pp. 10–27). See n. 18 to the Introduction.

478 Pelliot (1), 264–265, 321–348, and summary of his article in *BEFEO*, 21 (1922), 222–229. Cf. *HTS*, 222c, 4159d.

Hyŏnyu

Sŏk Hyŏnyu 釋玄遊[479] was a native of Koguryŏ. He was by nature other-wordly and harmonious,[480] affable and elegant. Determined to pursue the Dual Benefits, he had the ambition of searching for the truth. He could sail against the current in a cup or build a house in a dark ravine. When he went to T'ang and studied under the Dhyāna master Seng-che 僧哲,[481] he would lift up the hem of his robe whenever he received instructions.[482] Desiring to observe and admire the sacred traces, he sailed to the Western Regions, adapted his teaching to the new circumstances, and made extensive pilgrim-ages. He finally returned to eastern India, where he constantly learned from eminent monks and lived near them. Early in life he showed a marked pro-pensity for *Prajñā* and *Dhyāna*.[483] He probed the depths and fulfilled the mea-sure of the doctrine. He went forth empty-handed but returned heavily laden. Indeed, he was a pillar of the Buddhist school and a leader of the fellowship of monks.

Later, he regretted the fact that even as a boat hidden in the valley can disappear,[484] so also do mountains and valleys perpetually undergo change.[485] He also regretted the fact that there is no constancy in human life, that time flies by.[486] When the wood is consumed and the fire dies out, where can one obtain what is already spent? The master of the Tripiṭaka I-ching admired the unswerving loyalty to the Law [Hyŏnyu had displayed] from childhood. [Hyŏn]yu first demonstrated his piety in East China and later further sought the Law in India. He was delayed, because of other matters, in his return to China 神洲.[487] Propagating the ten practices of the Law,[488] he spread the

---

479 Appears as a Silla national in *CPT*, III, 205, line 9.
480 Cf. Chavannes (1), pp. 138–139.
481 *T*. 51, 8b-c (Chavannes [1], pp. 127–133).
482 The first logograph 哲 in the next sentence should be omitted.
483 In the original: 慧炬夙明，禪枝早茂.
484 舟壑潛移: *Nan-hua chen-ching*, 3, 8b-9a (Giles, *Chuang Tzu*, p. 75).
485 陵谷之遷質 or ———變: *Shih ching*, 193, 3 (Karlgren, p. 138).
486 居諸易脫: *Shih ching*, 26 (Karlgren, p. 16). A29a2 has 晚, which is wrong.
487 On 神州 (洲) as referring to China see Pelliot (3), 739, n. 2.
488 傳十法而弘法·十法 or 十種法行 (*daśa dharmacaryāḥ*): ten ways of devotion to the Buddhist

Law. He can live a thousand years and yet not die.[489] Although he died on foreign soil and could not return to the capital, his contribution was indeed great. It must be recorded in history and shown to posterity. [I-ching therefore] wrote the *Ch'iu-fa kao-seng chuan*. By chance I read the scriptures and came upon this paragraph. Deeply moved by his determination, I have made a selection [from his biography] and recorded it here.

---

sūtras. To dedicate and expound the scriptures is to spread the Dharma. See *Sheng-t'ien-wang po-jo-po-lo-mi ching* 勝天王般若波羅密經 7, *T*. 8, 725a8–12; *Prakaraṇāryavāca-śāstra* 顯揚聖教論 2, *T*. 31, 491a14 ff.

489 I.e., he is immortal as far as his fame is concerned.

Hyŏnt'ae

Sŏk Hyŏnt'ae 釋玄太 was a native of Silla. His name in Sanskrit was Sarvajña-deva, in Chinese, "Omniscient God" 一切智.[490] He was pensive as a child, and he had the marks *(lakṣaṇa)* of a great man *(Mahāpuruṣa)*.[491] He did not eat meat, nor. . . .[492]

He sailed to T'ang to study, and his learning was remarkable. He was able to explain the profound and to exhaust the subtle.[493] During the era *yung-huei* 永徽 (650–655) of Kao-tsung 高宗 (628–650–683) he went to Central India to pay homage to the bodhi tree. Like a lion in his roaming, he never sought any company. He brandished the golden staff with five towers[494] and saw the precious ladders of the Three Steps.[495] He braved hardships to make a tour of different places he longed to see,[496] yet he was unable to exhaust the Way.[497] Finally he stayed[498] in the Mahābodhi monastery, studied carefully the scriptures and treatises, and observed the local [1023a] customs. Later he returned to China to preach conversion to the Law, and his achievement was then well recognized. Great and lofty was his success![499]

The eulogy says: The several persons mentioned above are as remote from us as the easternmost extremity.[500] Going directly to the Middle

---

490 Chavannes (1), p. 34, n. 8. For his Sanskrit name, 薩婆愼菩提婆, read 若 for 菩 (天 not in A29b9). His Chinese name should be Hyŏnt'ae, as in I-ching's biography. *CPT*, III, 215, has Tae-bŏm 大梵 as his name, which is wrong.

491 Alex Wayman, "Contributions Regarding the Thirty-two Characteristics of the Great Person," *Sino-Indian Studies: Liebenthal Festschrift* (Santiniketan, 1957), pp. 243–260.

492 There is a lacuna of ten logographs in our text, but *CPT*, III, 205, has a lacuna of nine, preceded by 不 (嬉遊), making twelve altogether.

493 A29b1 reads 徵 for 微.

494 In the original: 五樓之金策.

495 三道之寶階. Once Buddha ascended to the Trāyastriṁśā Heaven and preached the Law for the sake of his mother Māyā. When he was about to descend, Śakra, king of the devas, erected three precious ladders for him, the center one of yellow gold, the left one of pure crystal, and the right one of white silver. See *T.* 51, 893a-b (Beal, *Si-yu-ki;* I, 202–204).

496 In *CPT*, III, 205, 其所遠冒難危, which makes better sense.

497 I follow *CPT*, III, 205, and read 道 for 導.

498 Literally, "he hung up his priestly staff."

499 A29b5 has 有 between 乎 and 成功.

500 青徼: *Wen hsüan*, 35, 89 (Von Zach, II, 638: "östliches Grenzland"). See *P'ei-wen yün-fu* 佩文韻府 *(WYWK)*, 4, 3111c.

Kingdom, they traced the steps of Fa-hsien and Hsüan-tsang. They went back and forth to the deserted regions, regarding them as lanes and streets. They can be compared with the envoys Chang Ch'ien 張騫[501] and Su Wu 蘇武.[502]

---

[501] See n. 36 to the Introduction.
[502] See n. 37 to the Introduction.

BIBLIOGRAPHY

This bibliography contains all the works cited in the notes except the Buddhist materials which are easily identifiable (e.g., *Shōwa hōbō sōmokuroku* [1929], *Taishō shinshū daizōkyō sōmokuroku* [1932], and "Tables du Taishō Issaikyō" in *HBGR* [1932]) and the works listed under "Abbreviations." Unless otherwise noted, all the Korean books are published in Seoul.

East Asian Sources

Adachi Kiroku. *Kōshō Hokken den* (Tokyo, 1936).
——— *Daitō saiiki guhō kōsōden* (Tokyo, 1942).
——— *Daitō saiiki ki* (Kyoto, 1942–1943).
An Kye-hyŏn. "P'algwanhoe ko," *Tongguk sahak*, 4 (1956), 31–54.
Araki Kengo. *Jukyō to bukkyō* (Kyoto, 1963).
Arimitsu Kyōichi. "Keishū Getsujō Taikyū Tatsujō no jōhekika no iseki ni tsuite," *CG*, 14 (1959), 489–502.
Chang Yü-shu et al. *K'ang-hsi tzu-tien* (*WYWK*).
——— *P'ei-wen yün-fu* (*WYWK*).
Ch'en Yin-k'o. "Ts'ui Hao yü K'ou Ch'ien-chi," *Ling-nan hsüeh-pao*, 11 (1950), 111–134.
Chi Yün et al. *Ssu-k'u ch'üan-shu tsung-mu* (Shanghai, 1930).
Ch'ien Mu, "Chung-kuo ssu-hsiang-shih chung-chih kuei-shen-kuan," *Hsin-ya hsüeh-pao*, 1 (1955), 1–43.
Chin Hong-sŏp. "Hŭngnyunsaji ch'ult'o ŭi wajŏn," *Kogo misul*, no. 59 (June 1965), 17–21.
Cho Chi-hun. "Silla kukho yŏn'gu non," *Koryŏ taehakkyo osip chunyŏn kinyŏm nonmunjip* (1955), pp. 167–188.
Cho Myŏng-gi. *Silla pulgyo ŭi inyŏm kwa yŏksa* (1962).
——— *Koryŏ Taegak kuksa wa Ch'ŏnt'ae sasang* (1964).
Ch'oe Cha. *Pohan chip* (*CKK*) (1911).

Ch'oe Kang-hyon. "Silla Sui chŏn sogo," *Kugŏ kungmunhak*, 25 (1962), 147–163; 26 (1963), 89–106.

Ch'oe Nam-sŏn. "Haedong kosŭng chŏn," *Pulgyo*, no. 37 (July 1927), 1–30.

—— "Shiragi Shinkōō no zairai sampi to shinshutsugen no Maunrei-hi," *SG*, 2 (1930), 69–90.

—— *Tonggyŏng t'ongji* (Kyŏngju, 1933).

Chŏng Chung-hwan. "Saro yukch'on kwa yukch'onin ŭi ch'ulsin e taehayŏ," *Yŏksa hakpo*, 17–18 (1962), 413–436.

Chŏng Yag-yong. *Chŏng Tasan chŏnsŏ* (3 vols.; 1960–1961).

Chou i (SPTK).

Chou li (SPTK).

Chu Ch'i-feng. *Tz'u t'ung* (Shanghai, 1934).

Chu-shu chi-nien (SPPY).

Eda Shunyū. "Shiragi no bukkyō juyō ni kansuru shomondai," *Bunka*, 2 (1935), 961–988.

—— "Shiragi no Jizō to Godaisan," *Bunka*, 21 (1957), 562–573.

—— "Shiragi no bukkyō," *Kōza bukkyō*, 4 (Tokyo, 1958), 253–278.

Ennin. *Nittō guhō junrei kōki* (*Dainihon bukkyō zensho*, 113; Tokyo, 1918).

Erh-shih-wu shih (K'ai-ming ed.).

Fang I et al. *Chung-kuo jen-ming ta-tz'u-tien* (Shanghai, 1934).

Fujita Ryōsaku. "Chōsen no nengō to kinen," *TG*, 41 (1958), 335–373:

Fujita Toyohachi. *Tōzai kōshōshi no kenkyū: Saiiki hen* (Tokyo, 1943).

Fukui Kōjun. *Tōyō shisōshi kenkyū* (Tokyo, 1960).

Fukunaga Mitsuji. "Shiton to sono shūi," *Bukkyō shigaku*, 5 (March 1956), 12–34.

Han Fei tzu (SPPY).

Han Ying. *Han-shih wai-chuan (SPTK)*.

Han Yü. *Ch'ang-li hsien -sheng chi (SPPY)*.

Hashimoto Hōkei. *Yuimagyō no shisōteki kenkyū* (Kyoto, 1966).

Hatani Ryōtai. *Saiiki no bukkyō* (Kyoto, 1914).

Hattori Masaaki. "Jinna oyobi sono shūhen no nendai," *Tsukamoto hakushi shōju kinen bukkyō shigaku ronshū* (Kyoto, 1961), pp. 79–96.

Hayashiya Tomojirō. *Bukkyō oyobi bukkyōshi no kenkyū* (Tokyo, 1948).

Hikata Ryūshō. "Seshin nendai saikō," *Miyamoto Shōson kyōju kanreki kinen rombunshū* (Tokyo, 1954), pp. 305–323.

Hong Sa-jun. "Silla Yŏngmyosaji ŭi ch'ujŏng," *Kogo misul*, no. 23 (June 1962), 5–10.

—— "Unmunsa ŭi Chagapchŏn," *Misul charyo*, 5 (1962), 11–14.

Hong Sun-t'ak. "Hyangyak kugŭppang ŏsa ko," *Honam munhwa yŏn'gu*, 2 (September 1964), 61–73.

Hoshikawa Kiyotaka. "Shindai ni okeru fūryū no rinen no seiritsu katei ni tsuite," *Ibaragi daigaku bunrigakubu kiyō*, 1 (1951), 93–104; 2 (1952), 100–114.

——— "Fūryū no shisō to Chūgoku bungaku," *Shibun*, 9 (1954), 11–25.

Hsiao T'ung. *Wen hsüan (WYWK)*.

Hsing-chün. *Lung-k'an shou-chien (SPTK)*.

Hsü Ching. *Hsüan-ho feng-shih Kao-li t'u-ching* (Keijō, 1932).

Hsü Shen. *Shuo wen (SPTK)*.

Hsün tzu (SPTK).

Hyech'o. *Wang o Ch'ŏnch'ukkuk chŏn* (Ch'oe Nam-sŏn ed.; 1954).

Hyŏngnyŏn Chŏng. *Kyunyŏ chŏn* (Ch'oe Nam-sŏn ed.; 1954).

Ikeda Suetoshi. "Kiji kō," *Hiroshima daigaku bungakubu kiyō*, 10 (1956), 206–248.

Ikeuchi Hiroshi. "Kōkuri kenkoku no densetsu to shijō no jijitsu," *TG*, 28 (1941), 169–189.

Imanishi Ryū. "Kaitō kōsō den," *SR*, 3 (July 1918), 452–458.

——— "Kōrai Fukaku kokuson Ichinen ni tsuikite," *Geimon*, 9 (1918), 601–616, 749–761.

——— "Shumō no densetsu oyobi Rōtatchi no densetsu," *Naitō hakushi shōju kinen shigaku ronsō* (Tokyo, 1930), pp. 715–741.

——— *Kōraishi kenkyū* (Keijō, 1944).

Izushi Yoshihiko. *Shina shinwa densetsu no kenkyū* (Tokyo, 1943).

Kagawa Yoshio. "Shōmangyō no kenkyū," *Bukkyō daigaku kenkyū kiyō*, 32 (1956), 47–82.

Kanaoka Shūyū. "Kongōmyōkyō no teiōkan to sono Shina-Nihonteki juyō," *Bukkyō shigaku*, 6 (1957), 267–278.

Kang Man-gil. "Chinhŭngwang pi ŭi suga myŏngsin yŏn'gu," *Sach'ong*, 1 (1955), 66–77.

Kim Ch'ŏl-chun. "Silla sangdae sahoe ŭi Dual Organization," *Yŏksa hakpo*, 1 (1952), 15–47; 2 (1952), 85–114.

Kim I-jae and Cho Pyŏng-gi. *Chunggyŏng chi (CKK)* (1911).

Kim Sang-gi. "Kalmunwang ko," *CH*, 5 (1936), 181–201.

——— "Taegak kuksa Ŭich'ŏn e taehayŏ," *Kuksasang ŭi chemunje*, 3 (1959), 79–102.

Kim Yŏng-t'ae. "Mirŭk sŏnhwa ko," *Pulgyo hakpo*, 3–4 (1966), 135–149.

Kimura Eiichi ed. *Eon kenkyū* (2 vols.; Kyoto, 1960–1962).

Ko Hung. *Pao-p'u tzu (WYWK)*.

Kobayashi Shimmei. "Wakōdōjin kō," *Tōhōgakkai sōritsu jūgoshūnen kinen Tōhōgaku ronshū* (Tokyo, 1962), pp. 105–115.

Konjaku monogatari shū (Nihon koten bungaku taikei, 23; Tokyo, 1960).

Ku Tsu-yü. *Tu-shih fang-yü chi-yao (WYWK)*.

Kuang-ya su-cheng (WYWK).

Kudō Jōshō. *Seshin kyōgaku no taikeiteki kenkyū* (Kyoto, 1955).

Kuwabara Jitsuzō. *Tōzai kōtsūshi ronsō* (Tokyo, 1944).

Kwŏn Che et al. *Yongbi ŏch'ŏn ka* (Kyujanggak series, 4–5; Keijō, 1937–1938).

Kwŏn Kŭn. *Yangch'on chip* (1937 ed.).

Kwŏn Mun-hae. *Taedong unbu kunok (Kukko ch'ongsŏ,* 1; 1950).

Kwŏn Sang-no. "Han'guk kodae sinang ŭi illyŏn," *Pulgyo hakpo,* 1 (1963), 81–108.

Li chi (SPPY).

Li-chi chu-su (SPPY).

Li Fang et al. *T'ai-p'ing yü-lan* (1807 ed.).

Li Po. *Ri Haku no sakuhin (Tōdai kenkyū no shiori,* 9; Kyoto, 1958).

Lieh tzu (SPPY).

Ling-fu Ch'eng. *Ta-chung i-shih (Shuo-fu,* 49).

Liu I-ch'ing. *Shih-shuo hsin-yü (SPPY).*

Lun yü (Harvard-Yenching Institute Sinological Index Series, Supplement No. 16).

Matsumoto Bunsaburō. "Butten ni arawaruru Shintan no go ni tsuite," *SR,* 12 (1927), 36–45, 179–191.

Meng tzu (Harvard-Yenching Institute Sinological Index Series, Supplement No. 17).

Mishina Shōei. "Kodai Chōsen ni okeru ōja shutsugen no shinwa to girei ni tsuite," *SR,* 18 (1933), 67–96, 328–371, 453–480.

——— "Chōsen ni okeru bukkyō to minzoku shinkō," *Bukkyō shigaku,* 4 (1954), 9–33.

Mitamura Taisuke. "Shumō no densetsu to Tsungūsu bunka no seikaku," *Ritsumeikan bungaku,* 70–72 (Kyoto, 1949), 97–117.

Miyakawa Hisayuki. *Rikuchōshi kenkyū* (Tokyo, 1956).

Miyamoto Shōson. "Shōjo shuron no kenkyū: Tendai Kajō ni okeru Shina bukkyō no ichimondai," *Bukkyō kenkyū,* 2 (Tokyo, 1938), 1–32.

Mori Mikisaburō. *Ryō no Butei* (Kyoto, 1956).

Moroto Tatsuo. "Yō Kō no sūfutsu to Rajū no yakkyō jigyō," *Tōyōgaku,* 6 (Sendai, 1961), 35–48.

Murakami Yoshimi. "Kōsōden no shini ni tsuite," *Tōhō shūkyō,* 17 (1961), 1–17.

Nagasawa Yōji. "Kodai Chūgoku ni okeru kijin no imi ni tsuite," *Fukushima daigaku gakugeigakubu ronshū,* 1 (1950), 71–94.

Naitō Shunpo. *Chōsen-shi kenkyū* (Kyoto, 1961).

Nakamura Hajime and Kawada Kumatarō, eds. *Kegon shisō* (Kyoto, 1960).

Nan-hua chen-ching (SPTK).

Ninomiya Keinin. "Kōrai no Hakkane ni tsukite," *CG,* 9 (1956), 235–251.

——— "Chōsen ni okeru Ninnōe no kaisetsu," *CG,* 14 (1959), 155–163.

——— "Kōraichō no kōrei hōe," *CG,* 15 (1960), 19–30.

Nomura Yōshō. *Sangoku iji (Kokuyaku issaikyō,* Shidenbu 10; 1962), pp. 251–635.

Ŏ Suk-kwŏn. *P'aegwan chapki (CKK;* 1904).

Ōchō Enichi. *Chūgoku bukkyō no kenkyū* (Kyoto, 1958).

Ogawa Tamaki. "Fūryū no gogi no henka," *Kokugo kokubun,* 20 (1951), 514–526.

——— *Tōshi gaisetsu* (Tokyo, 1958).

Ōta Teizō. "Ryō Butei no shadō hōfutsu ni tsuite utgau," *Yūki kyōju shōju kinen bukkyō shisōshi ronshū* (Tokyo, 1964), pp. 417–432.

Ōtani Kōshō. "Tōdai bukkyō no girei: tokuni hōe ni tsuite," *SZ*, 46 (1935), 1183–1231, 1377–1405.

Ōtani Kunihiko. "Chūgoku kodai no tenseki ni okeru shin to ki," *Kambungaku kenkyū*, 11 (1963), 1–11; *Chūgoku koten kenkyū*, 12 (1964), 83–96.

Ōya Tokujō. *Kōrai zokuzō chūzōkō* (3 vols.; Kyoto, 1937).

Pak Pong-u. "Ch'ŏnggu sŭngjŏn poram," *Shin pulgyo*, nos. 21–27 (February-November, 1940).

Po-hu t'ung (SPTK).

Sakamoto Yukio. *Kegon kyōgaku no kenkyū* (Kyoto, 1956).

Sasaki Gesshō. *Kan'yaku shihon taishō, Shōdaijōron tsuki Chibetto yaku Shōdaijōron* (Tokyo, 1959).

Satō Tetsuei. "Hokke gengi no seiritsu katei ni kansuru kenkyū," *Indogaku bukkyō-gaku kenkyū*, 6 (1958), 312–322.

Shan-hai ching (SPTK).

Shang shu (SPTK).

Shih ching (Harvard-Yenching Institute Sinological Index Series, Supplement No. 9).

Sŏ Kŏ-jŏng. *Tongin sihwa* (CKK; 1911).

——— *Tongmun sŏn* (CKK; 1914).

Son Chin-t'ae. "China minjok ŭi unggye sinang kwa kŭ chŏnsŏl," *CH*, 3 (1935), 76–92.

Ssu-ma Kuang. *Tzu-chih t'ung-chien* (Peking, 1957).

Suematsu Yasukazu. *Shiragi-shi no shomondai* (Tokyo, 1954).

Sugano no Mamichi. *Shoku Nihongi* (Shintei zōho kokushi taikei, 2; Tokyo, 1937).

Sugimoto Naojirō and Mitarai Masaru. "Kodai Chūgoku ni okeru taiyō setsuwa," *Minzokugaku kenkyū*, 15 (1950), 304–327.

Sung Min-ch'iu. *Ch'ang-an chih (Tōdai kenkyū no shiori*, 6; Kyoto, 1956).

Suzuki Keizō. "Kōtei sunawachi Bosatsu to Kōtei sunawachi Nyorai ni tsuite," *Bukkyō shigaku*, 10 (1962), 1–15.

Suzuki Munetada. *Yuishiki tetsugaku kenkyū* (Kyoto, 1957).

Taegak kuksa munjip (1931).

Takahashi Tōru. "Daikaku kokushi no Kōrai bukkyō ni taisuru keirin ni tsuite," *CG*, 10 (1956), 113–147.

——— *Richō bukkyō* (Tokyo, 1929).

Takamine Ryōshū. *Kegon shisōshi* (Kyoto, 1963).

Takigawa Kametarō. *Shiki kaichū kōshō* (10 vols.; Tokyo, 1933–1935).

Tamura Sennosuke. "Shiro no rokuson to sono Shiragi eno hatten," *SG*, 28 (1937), 82–125.

T'ang Yung-t'ung. *Han-Wei liang-Chin Nan-pei-ch'ao fo-chiao-shih* (2 vols.; Shanghai, 1938).

Ting Fu-pao. *Fo-hsüeh ta-tz'u-tien* (Shanghai, 1921).

Tokiwa Daijō. *Memyō bosatsu ron* (Tokyo, 1905).

Tongguk taehakkyo bulgyo sahak yon'gusil, ed. *Tongsa yŏlchŏn (Changwoe chamnok,* 2; 1957).

Tsang Li-ho et al. *Chung-kuo ku-chin ti-ming ta-tz'u-tien* (Shanghai, 1930).

Tso chuan (Harvard-Yenching Institute Sinological Index Series, Supplement No. 11).

Tsuboi Shunei. "Kanazawa bunko shozō Enshū monrui narabini kaidai," *Butsudai gakuhō,* 30 (1955), 99–121.

Tsukamoto Zenryū. *Shina bukkyōshi kenkyū: Hokugi hen* (Tokyo, 1942).

———, ed. *Jōron kenkyū* (Kyoto, 1955).

———, "Chūgoku no bukkyō hakugai," *Kōza bukkyō,* 4 (Tokyo, 1958), 131–164.

Tu Fu. *Tu Shao-ling chi hsiang-chu (WYWK).*

Tu Yu. *T'ung tien* (Kuo-hsüeh chi-pen ts'ung-shu ed.; Taipei, 1959).

Tung Tso-pin. *Chronological Tables of Chinese History* (2 vols.; Hong Kong, 1960).

Ui Hakuju. *Shōdaijōron no kenkyū* (Tokyo, 1935).

——— "Shōmangyō no bonbun danpen," *Nagoyadaigaku bungakubu jisshūnen kinen ronshū* (1954), pp. 189–210.

——— *Daijō butten no kenkyū* (Tokyo, 1963).

Wang Ch'in-jo et al. *Ts'e-fu yüan-kuei* (Chung-hua shu-chü ed.; 1960).

Wang Ch'ung. *Lun heng (SPPY).*

Wang P'u. *T'ang hui-yao (TSCC).*

Wang Su. *K'ung-tzu chia-yu (SPPY).*

Wei Ying-wu. *Wei Chiang-chou chi (SPTK).*

Yamada Ryūjō. *Bongo butten no shobunken* (Tokyo, 1959).

Yamanouchi Shinkyō. *Shina bukkyōshi no kenkyū* (Kyoto, 1921).

Yamasaki Hiroshi. "Ryō Butei no bukkyō shinkō ni tsuite," *Saitō sensei koki kinen shukuga ronshū* (Tokyo, 1937), pp. 437–470.

Yang Chu-dong. *Koga yŏn'gu* (1957).

Yang Lien-sheng. "Lao-chün yin-sung chieh-ching chiao-shih," *Chung-yang yen-chiu-yüan li-shih yü-yen yen-chiu-so chi-k'an,* 28 (1956), 17–54.

Yang Po-chün. *Lieh-tzu chi-shih* (Shanghai, 1958).

Yaotani Takayasu. "Shiragi shakai to Jōdokyō," *Shichō,* 7 (1937), 609–658.

——— "Shiragisō Gishō-den kō," *Shina bukkyō shigaku,* 3 (1939), 79–94.

Yi Chae-ch'ang. "Samguk sagi bulgyo ch'ojon puju," *Pulgyo hakpo,* 2 (1964), 305–322.

Yi Hong-jik, ed. *Kuksa taesajŏn* (2 vols.; 1963).

Yi Hye-gu. "Ŭiryesang ŭro pon P'algwanhoe," *Yesul nonmunjip,* 1 (1962), 92–108.

Yi Il-lo. *Kugyok P'ahan chip* (1964).

Yi Ki-baek. "Samguk sidae pulgyo chŏllae wa kŭ sahoejŏk sŏngkyŏk," *Yŏksa hakpo,*

6 (1954), 128–205.

Yi Ki-mun. "Sipsam segi chungyŏp ŭi kugŏ charyo: Hyangyak kugŭppang ŭi kach'i," *Tonga munhwa*, 1 (1963), 63–91.

Yi Kyu-bo. *Tongguk Yisangguk chip (KKH;* 1958).

Yi Kyu-gyŏng. *Oju yŏnmun changjŏn san'go (KKH;* 1959).

Yi Pyŏng-do. "Chindan pyŏn," *CH,* 1 (1934), 167–174.

——— "Imsin sŏgi sŏk e taehayŏ," *Seoul taehakkyo nonmunjip*, 5 (1957), 1–7.

——— *Han'guk sa,* I (1959); II (1962).

Yi Pyŏng-ju. "Sŏkpo sangjŏl che isipsam isipsa haeje," *Tongak ŏmun nonjip*, 5 (1967), 1–106.

Yi Su-gwang. *Chibong yusŏl (CKK;* 1909).

Yi Sŭng-hyu. *Chewang un'gi* (Ch'oe Nam-sŏn ed.; 1958).

Yi U-sŏng. "Koryŏ chunggi ŭi minjok sŏsasi: Tongmyŏngwang p'yŏn kwa Chewang un'gi ŭi yŏn'gu," *Sŏnggyungwan taehakkyo nonmunjip*, 7 (1962), 84–117.

Yoshikawa Buntarō. *Chōsen no shūkyō* (Keijō, 1921).

Yu Ch'ang-don. *Yijoŏ sajŏn* (1964).

Yūki Reimon. *Seshin yuishiki no kenkyū* (Tokyo, 1955).

——— *Yuishikigaku tensekishi* (Tokyo, 1962).

Western Sources

Ashikaga, Enshō. "Notes on Urabon (Yü Lan P'en)," *JAOS,* 71 (1961), 71–75.

Aurousseau, Léonard. "La première conquête chinoise des pays annamites, IIIe siècle avant notre ère," *BEFEO,* 23 (1923), 137–264.

Bareau, André. *Les sectes bouddhiques du petit véhicule* (Saigon, 1955).

Beal, Samuel. *Travels of Fah-Hian and Sung Yün, Buddhist Pilgrims from China to India* (London, 1869).

——— *Si-yu-ki, Buddhist Records of the Western World* (2 vols.; London, 1906).

Biot, Édouard. *Le Tcheou-li ou Rites des Tcheou* (3 vols.; Peiping, 1930).

Bynner, Witter. *The Jade Mountain* (New York, 1929).

Chan, Wing-tsit. "Transformation of Buddhism in China," *Philosophy East and West,* 7 (1958), 107–116.

——— *A Source Book in Chinese Philosophy* (Princeton, 1963).

Chapin, Helen B. "Yünnanese Images of Avalokiteśvara," *HJAS,* 8 (1944), 131–186.

Chavannes, Édouard. *Documents sur les Tou-kiue (turcs) occidentaux* (Paris, n.d.).

——— *Cinq cents contes et apologues extraits du Tripiṭaka chinois* (4 vols.; Paris, 1910–1934).

Ch'en, Kenneth K. S. "A Study of the Svāgata Story in the Divyāvadāna in Its Sanskrit, Pāli, Tibetan, and Chinese Versions," *HJAS,* 9 (1947), 207–314.

———— "Anti-Buddhist Propaganda during the Nan-ch'ao," *HJAS*, 15 (1952), 166–192.

———— *Buddhism in China: A Historical Survey* (Princeton, 1964).

Clifford, James L., ed. *Biography as an Art* (New York, 1962).

Chou, Yi-liang. "Tantrism in China," *HJAS*, 8 (1945), 241–332.

Conze, Edward. *The Prajñāpāramitā Literature* (The Hague, 1960).

Couvreur, Séraphin. *Li Ki ou Mémoires sur les Bienséances et les Cérémonies* (2 vols.; Hokienfou, 1913).

Creel, H. G. *Confucius, the Man and the Myth* (New York, 1945).

———— "What is Taoism?" *JAOS*, 76 (1956), 139–152.

Davis, A.R., ed. *The Penguin Book of Chinese Verse* (Harmondsworth, 1965).

Dayal, Har. *The Bodhisattva Doctrine in Buddhist Sanskrit Literature* (London, 1932).

de Mallmann, Marie Thérèse. *Étude iconographique sur Mañjuśrī* (Paris, 1964).

de Visser, M. W. *Ancient Buddhism in Japan* (2 vols.; Leiden, 1935).

———— *The Dragon in China and Japan* (Amsterdam, 1913).

Demiéville, Paul. "Les versions chinoises du Milindapañha," *BEFEO*, 24 (1924), 1–253.

———— *Le Concile de Lhasa* (Paris, 1952).

———— "La pénétration du bouddhisme dans la tradition philosophique chinoise," *Cahiers d'Histoire Mondiale*, 3 (1956), 19–38.

des Rotours, Robert. *Traité des fonctionnaires et Traité de l'armée* (2 vols.; Leiden, 1947–1948).

Dien, A. E. " 'Chiang-yu/chiang-tso': Right and Left of the Yangtze; A problem in Historical Geography," *JAOS*, 82 (1962), 376–383.

Dodds, E. R. *The Greeks and the Irrational* (Berkeley and Los Angeles, 1951).

Dschi, Hian-lin. "Lieh-tzu and Buddhist Sutras," *Studia Serica*, 9 (1950), 18–32.

Dubs, Homer H. *The Works of Hsüntze* (London, 1928).

———— *The History of the Former Han Dynasty* (3 vols.; Baltimore, 1938–1955).

Duyvendak, J.J.L. *Tao Te Ching: The Book of the Way and Its Virtue* (London, 1954).

Ecke, Gustav and Paul Demiéville. *The Twin Pagodas of Zayton* (Cambridge, 1935).

Eliot, T. S. *The Use of Poetry and the Use of Criticism* (Cambridge, Mass., 1933).

Fisher, Jakob and Yokota Takezo. *Das Sūtra Vimalakirti: Das Sūtra über die Erlösung* (Tokyo, 1944).

Forke, Alfred. *Lun heng. Philosophical Essays of Wang Ch'ung* (2 vols.; London, 1907).

Foucher, Alfred. "Notes sur l'itinéraire de Hiuan-Tsang en Afghanistan," *Études Asiatiques publiées à l'occasion du vingt-cinquième anniversaire de l'École Française d'Extrême-Orient*, 1 (1925), 257–284.

Franke, Otto. *Geschichte des chinesischen Reiches* (5 vols.; Berlin and Leipzig, 1930–1952).

Frauwallner, Erich. *On the Date of the Buddhist Master of the Law Vasubandhu* (Rome,

1951).

Frodsham, J. D. "Hsieh Ling-yün's Contribution to Medieval Chinese Buddhism," International Association of Historians of Asia, *Proceedings of the Second Biennial Congress* (1962), pp. 27–55.

Fuchs, Walter. "Huei-ch'ao's Pilgerreise durch Nordwest-Indien und Zentral-Asien um 726," *Sitzungsberichte der Preussischen Akademie der Wissenschaften*, Philosophisch-historische Klasse, 30 (Berlin, 1938), 426–469.

Fung, Yu-lan. *A History of Chinese Philosophy*, I (London,1952), II (Princeton, 1953).

Giles, Herbert A. *The Travels of Fa-Hsien* (Cambridge, 1923).

——— *Chuang Tzu* (London, 1961).

Graham, A.C. *The Book of Lieh-tzu* (London, 1960).

——— "The Date and Composition of Liehtzyy," *AM*, 8 (1961), 139–198.

Grousset, René. *In the Footsteps of the Buddha* (London, 1932).

Haguenauer, Charles. "Le 'ki-kouei' de Yi-tsing et le 'kye-rim' de l'histoire," *Kano kyōju kanreki kinen Shinagaku ronsō* (Kyoto, 1928), pp. 13–25.

Hightower, James, R. *Han Shih Wai Chuan* (Cambridge, 1952).

Hikata, Ryūshō. *Suvikrāntavikrami pariprcchā Prajñāpāramitā-sūtra* (Fukuoka, 1958).

Hirth, Frederick. "The Story of Chang Ch'ien, China's Pioneer in West Asia," *JAOS*, 37 (1917), 89–152.

Hung, William. *Tu Fu* (Cambridge, 1952).

Hurvitz, Leon. *Chih-I (538–597): An Introduction to the Life and Ideas of a Chinese Buddhist Monk. MCB*, 12 (1962).

Izumi, Hōkei. "Vimalakirti's Discourse on Emancipation," *The Eastern Buddhist*, 2 (1922–1923), 358–366; 3 (1924–1925), 55–69, 138–153, 224–242, 336–349; 4 (1926–1928), 48–55, 177–190, 348–366.

Japanese-English Buddhist Dictionary (Tokyo, 1965).

Jones, S. W., tr. *Ages Ago: Thirty-Seven Tales from the Konjaku Monogatari Collection* (Cambridge, 1959).

Julien, Stanislas. *Voyages de Pèlerins Bouddhistes* (vols. II–III; Paris, 1853–1858).

Karlgren, Bernhard. *The Book of Odes* (Stockholm, 1950).

Kendall, Paul Murray. *The Art of Biography* (New York, 1965).

Kern, Hendrik. *The Saddharma-Puṇḍarika or the Lotus of the True Law* (Oxford, 1884).

Kim, Chewon and Won-yong Kim. *Treasures of Korean Art: 2000 Yearas of Ceramics, Sculptures, and Jeweled Arts* (New York, 1966).

Kramers, R. P. *K'ung Tzu Chia Yu: The School Sayings of Confucius* (Leiden, 1950).

La Vallée Poussin, Louis de. *L'Abhidharmakośa de Vasubandhu* (6 vols.; Paris and Louvain, 1923–1931).

Lamotte, Étienne. *La Somme du Grand Véhicule d'Asaṅga* (Louvain, 1938–1939).

——— *Histoire du Bouddhisme Indien, des Origines a l'ère Śaka* (Louvain, 1958).

——— "Mañjuśrī," *TP*, 48 (1960), 1–96.

———— *L'Enseignement de Vimalakīrti* (Louvain, 1962).

Laufer, Bertold. "Optical Lenses," *TP*, 16 (1915), 169–228.

Law, Bimala Churn. *Geography of Early Buddhism* (London, 1932).

Lee, Ki-moon. "A Comparative Study of Manchu and Korean," *Ural-Altaische Jahrbücher*, 30 (1958), 104–120.

Lee, Peter H. *Studies in the Saenaennorae: Old Korean Poetry* (Rome, 1959).

———— *Anthology of Korean Poetry* (New York, 1964).

———— *Korean Literature: Topics and Themes* (Tucson, 1965).

Lévi, Sylvain. "Notes sur les Indo-scythes," *JA*, 9th series, 8 (1896), 444–484; 9 (1897), 5–42.

Liebenthal, Walter. "Shih Hui-yüan's Buddhism as set forth in His Writings," *JAOS*, 70 (1950), 243–259.

———— "New Light on the Mahāyāna-śraddhopāda śāstra," *TP*, 46 (1958), 155–216.

Link, Arthur E. "Biography of Shih Tao-an," *TP*, 46(1958), 1–48.

———— "Shih Seng-yü and his Writings," *JAOS*, 80 (1960), 17–43.

———— "Cheng-wu lun: The Rectification of Unjustified Criticism," *Oriens Extremus*, 8 (1961), 136–165.

Masuda, Jiryō. 'Origin and Doctrines of Early Indian Buddhist Schools," *AM*, 2 (1925), 1–78.

Menschen-Helfen, Otto. "The Yüeh-chih Problem Re-examined," *JAOS*, 65 (1945), 71–81.

Miller, Roy Andrew. *Accounts of Western Nations in the History of the Northern Chou Dynasty* (Berkeley and Los Angeles, 1959).

Needham, Joseph. *Science and Civilization in China*, I (Cambridge, 1954), II (1956), III (1959).

Nobel, Johannes. "Kumārajīva," *Sitzungsberichte der Preussischen Akademie der Wissenschaften*, 20 (1927), 206–233.

———— *Suvarnaprabhāsottama-sūtra* (2 vols.; Leiden, 1958).

Obata, Shigeyoshi. *The Works of Li Po* (Tokyo, 1935).

Ogihara, Unrai. *Bonwa Daijiten* (Tokyo, 1940–1943, 1963–1966).

Payne, Robert, ed. *The White Pony* (London, 1949).

Péri, Noel. "A propos de la date de Vasubandhu," *BEFEO*, 11 (1911), 339–390.

Petech, Luciano. *Northern India According to the Shui-ching-chu* (Rome, 1950).

Przyluski, Jean. *La Légende de l'Empereur Açoka* (Paris, 1923).

Rawski, Conrad H., tr. *Petrarch: Four Dialogues for Scholars* (Cleveland, 1967).

Reischauer, Edwin O. *Ennin's Diary* (New York, 1955).

Renou, Louis and Jean Filliozat, *L'Inde Classique*, II (Hanoi and Paris, 1953).

Richard, Timothy. *Ashvagosha, The Awakening of Faith* (London, 1961).

Robinson, Richard H. "Some Logical Aspects of Nāgārjuna's System," *Philosophy East and West*, 6 (1957), 291–308.

—— *Early Mādhyamika in India and China* (Madison, 1967).

Ryagaloff, A. "Dissertation sur le montage et le doublage," *JA*, 236 (1948), 103–113.

Schafer, E. H. "The Auspices of T'ang," *JAOS*, 83 (1963), 197–224.

Schlegel, Gustaaf. *Uranographie Chinoise* (2 vols.; Leiden, 1875).

—— "Fou-sang kouo," *TP*, A3 (1892), 101–168.

—— "Wen-chin kouo," *TP*, A3 (1892), 490–494.

Shiratori, Kurakichi. "The Legend of the King Tung-ming, the Founder of the Fu-yu-kuo," *MTB*, 10 (1938), 1–39.

—— "The Geography of the Western Regions: Studies on the Basis of the Ta-Ch'in Accounts," *MTB*, 15 (1956), 73–167.

—— "On the Ts'ung-ling Traffic Route Described by C. Ptolemaeus," *MTB*, 16 (1957), 1–34.

Soothill, W. E. *The Lotus of the Wonderful Law* (Oxford, 1930).

Soper, Alexander. "Northern Liang and Northern Wei in Kansu," *Artibus Asiae*, 21 (1958), 131–164.

Stein, Sir Aurel. *Ancient Khotan* (2 vols.; Oxford, 1907).

—— *Serindia* (3 vols.; Oxford, 1921).

Suzuki, D. T. *Studies in the Laṅkāvatāra Sūtra* (London, 1930).

Takakusu, Junjirō. *A Record of the Buddhist Religion as Practised in India and the Malay Archipelago by I-Tsing* (Oxford, 1896).

—— "The Life of Vasu-bandhu by Paramārtha (A.D. 499–569)," *TP*, 5 (1904), 269–296.

T'ang, Yung-t'ung. "On Ko-yi, the Earliest Method by which Indian Buddhism and Chinese Thought were Synthesized," *Radhakrishnan: Comparative Study in Philosophy* (London, 1951), pp. 276–286.

Tjan, Tjoe Som. *Po Hu T'ung: The Comprehensive Discussions in the White Tiger Hall* (2 vols.; Leiden, 1949–1952).

Tsukamoto, Zenryū. "The Śramaṇa Superintendant T'an-yao and His Time," *Monumenta Serica*, 16 (1957), 363–396.

Université de Paris Centre franco-chinois d'études sinologiques. *Index du Chan Hai King* (Peiping, 1948).

Viennot, Odette. *Le culte de l'arbre dans l'Inde ancienne* (Paris, 1954).

Von Zach, Erwin. *Han Yü's Poetische Werke* (Cambridge, 1952).

—— *Tu Fu's Gedichte* (2 vols.; Cambridge, 1952).

—— *Die Chinesische Anthologie* (2 vols.; Cambridge, 1958).

Waley, Arthur. *The Analects of Confucius* (London, 1949).

—— *The Real Tripitaka* (London, 1952).

—— *The Book of Songs* (London, 1954).

—— *The Way and Its Power* (London, 1956).

Walleser, Max. "The Life of Nāgārjuna from Tibetan and Chinese Sources," *AM*,

Hirth Anniversary Volume (1922), 421–455.

Ware, James R. "Wei Shou on Buddhism," *TP*, 30 (1933), 100–181.

———— "The Wei shu and the Sui shu on Taoism," *JAOS*, 53 (1933), 215–250.

Watson, Burton. *Ssu-ma Ch'ien: Grand Historian of China* (New York, 1958).

———— *Records of the Grand Historian of China* (2 vols.; New York, 1961).

———— *Han Fei Tzu: Basic Writings* (New York, 1964).

———— *Chuang Tzu: Basic Writings* (New York, 1964).

Watters, Thomas. *On Yuan Chwang's Travels in India 629–645* A.D. (2 vols.; London, 1904–1905).

Wayman, Alex. "Contributions Regarding the Thirty-two Characteristics of the Great Person," *Sino-Indian Studies: Liebenthal Festschrift* (Santiniketan, 1957), pp. 243–260.

Werner, E.T.C. *A Dictionary of Chinese Mythology* (Shanghai, 1932).

White, Helen C. *Tudor Books of Saints and Martyrs* (Madison, 1963).

Wilhelm, Richard. *The I Ching or Book of Changes* (2 vols.; New York, 1950).

Wright, Arthur F. "Fo-t'u-teng," *HJAS*, 11 (1948), 321–371.

———— "Hui-chiao's *Lives of Eminent Monks*," *Silver Jubilee Volume of Zinbun Kagaku Kenkyūjo* (Kyoto, 1954), pp. 383–432.

———— "Buddhism and Chinese Culture: Phases of Interaction," *JAS*, 17 (1957), 17–42.

Wright, Arthur F. and Denis Twitchett, eds. *Confucian Personalities* (Stanford, 1962).

Index